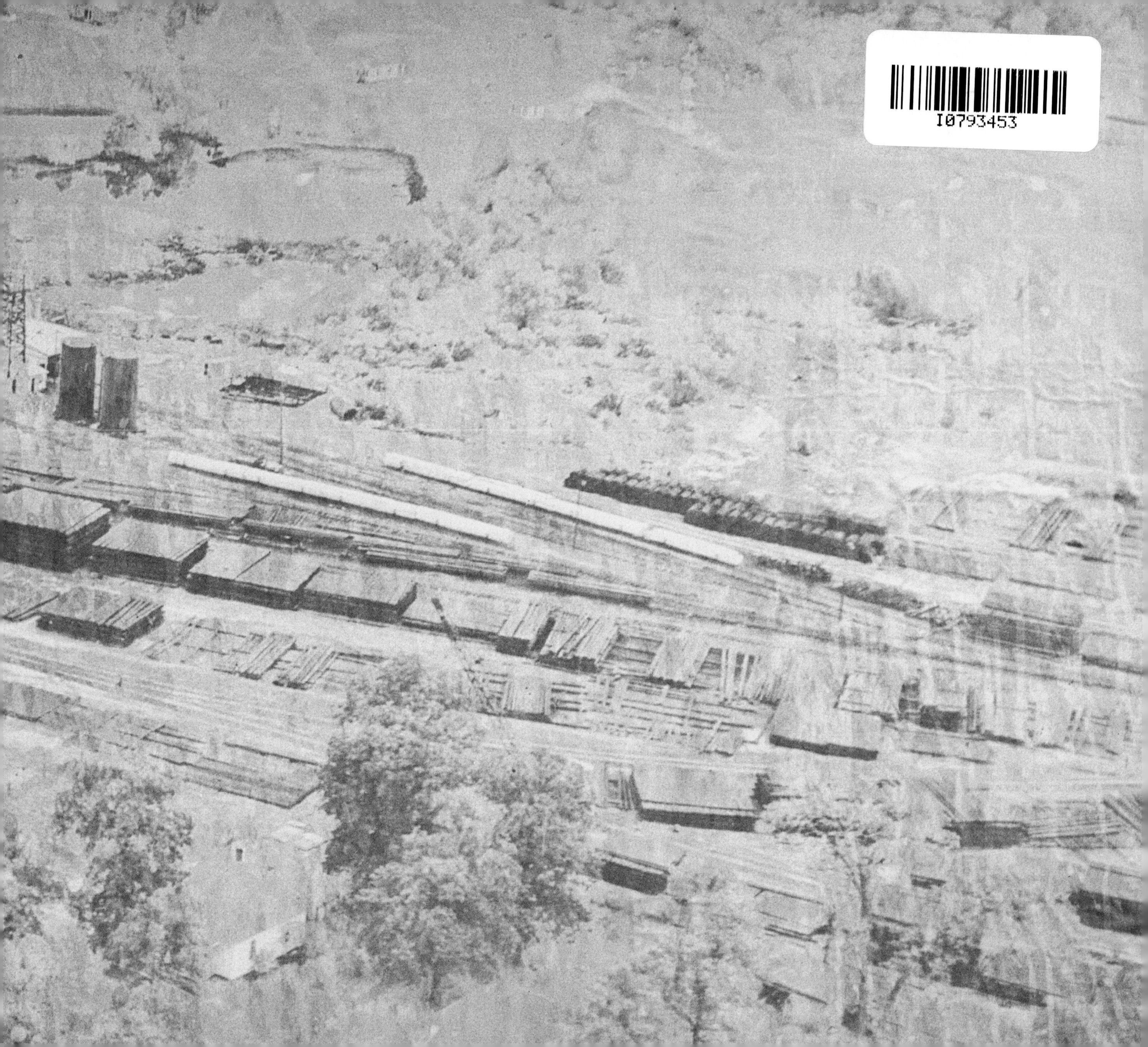

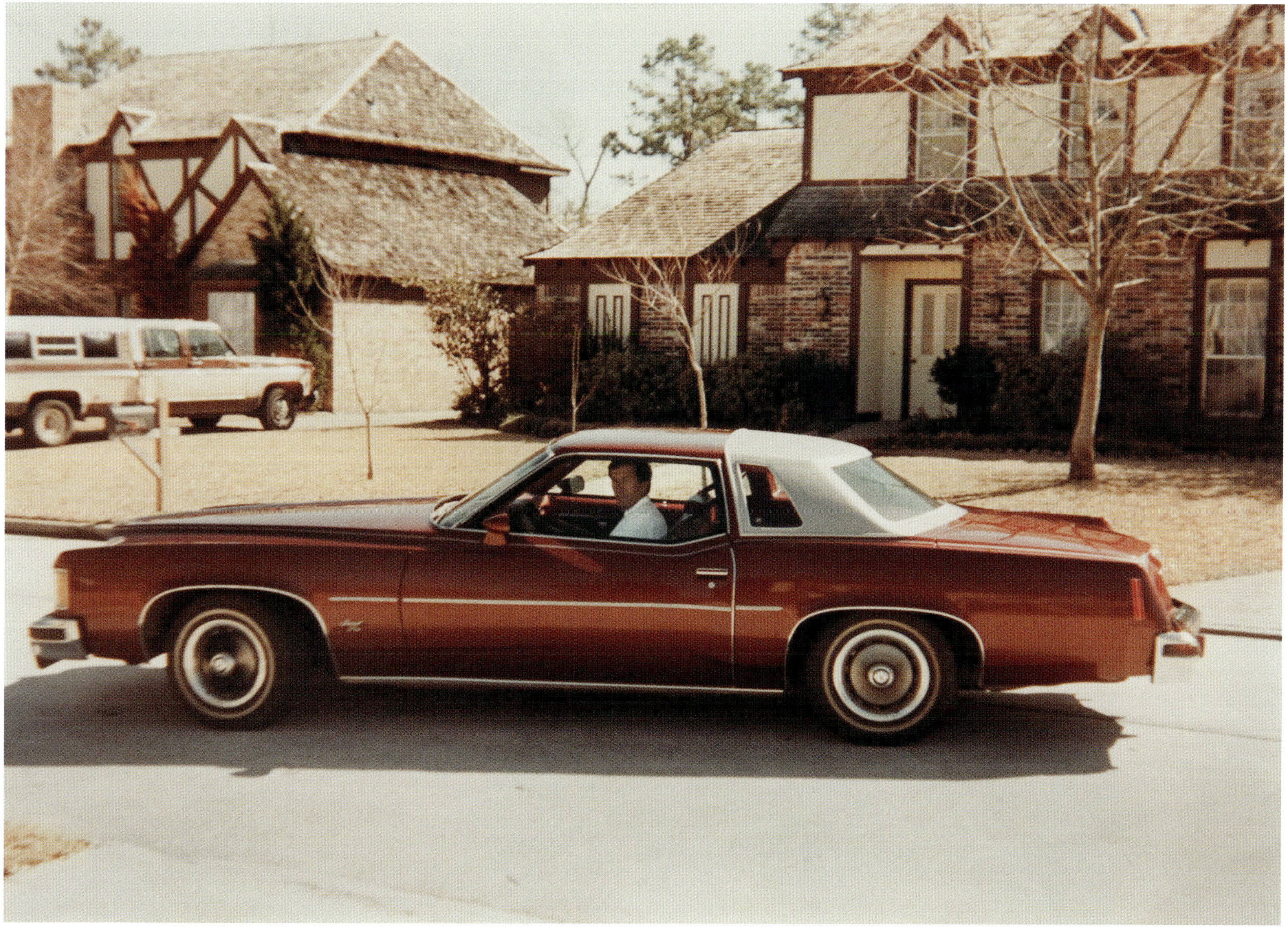

Daylight

Editors: Taj Forer and Michael Itkoff
Design: Ursula Damm
Copyediting: Dianne Timblin

ISBN 978-0-9889831-1-3

Printed in China

Daylight Books

E-mail: info@daylightbooks.org

Web: www.daylightbooks.org

MAY THE ROAD RISE TO MEET YOU

SARA MACEL

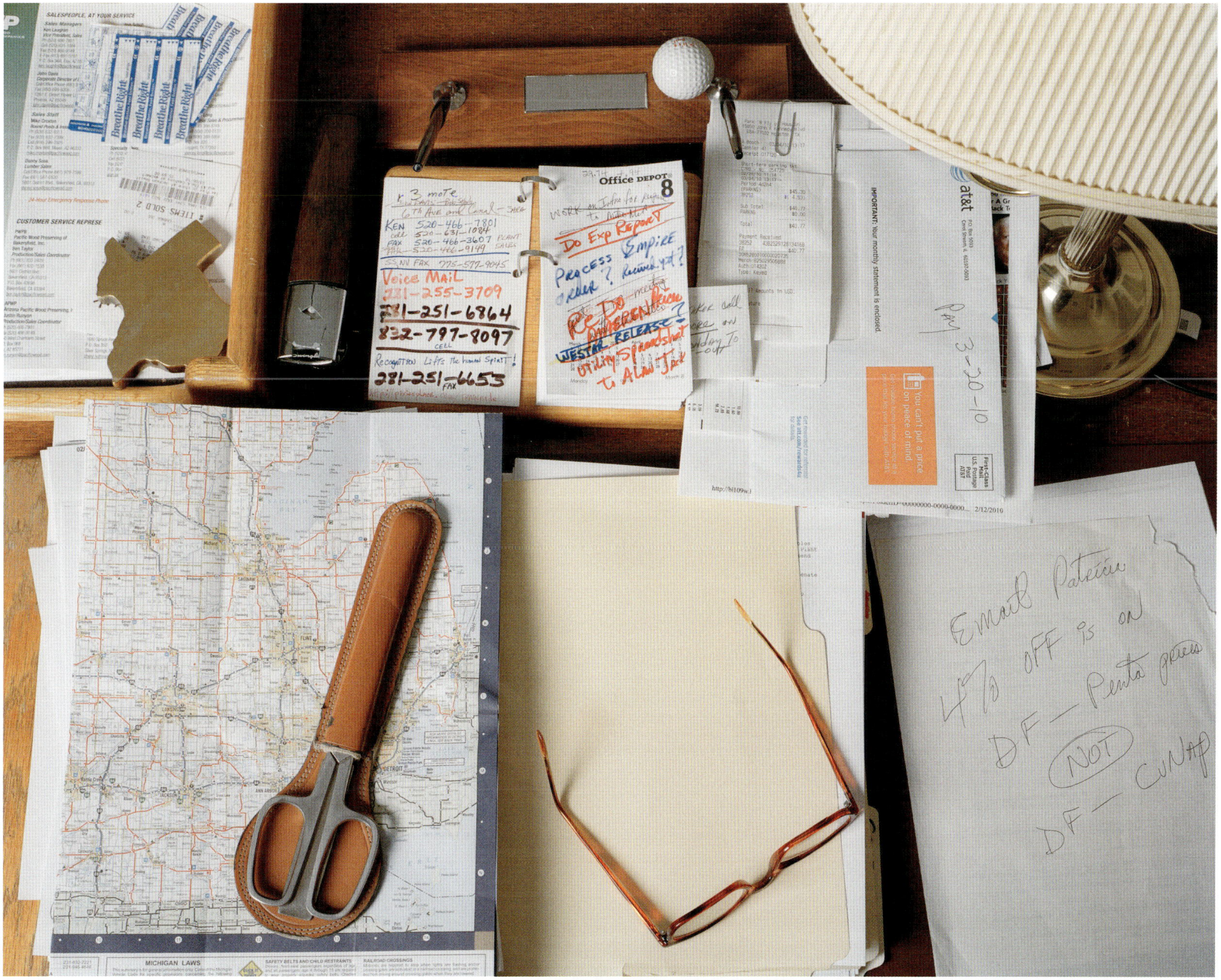

Office DEPOT 8
Do Exp Report
Voice Mail
281-255-3709
281-251-6864
832-797-8097
281-251-6653
at&t
IMPORTANT: Your monthly statement is enclosed.
You can't put a price on peace of mind.
MICHIGAN LAWS

ON THE ROAD. AGAIN.

—Marvin Heiferman

Work is something most people don't want or need pictures of. The office may be a popular setting for sitcoms, but it's seldom the subject of the snapshots or art we want to look at twice. We walk right by the head shots of smiling employees-of-the-month in the entryways of big-box stores. Photographs of the workplace are seldom ennobled by picture frames or places of honor on walls, night tables, or mantelpieces. Work, for many, is just work, the means to an end. Even if it's enjoyable, we don't like being reminded of where we are programmed to go most days, the routine things we do once we arrive, or the cast of characters we're compelled to engage with.

Why make or look at photographs of that?

There are, of course, plenty of reasons. Work, for some, can be self-defining and satisfying, something to be proud of. Work can be the opposite, a place that needs to be surveilled in order to uncover what would otherwise go unseen. CEOs, humanitarians, whistle-blowers, stock photo agencies, and journalists have all, historically, had their various reasons to document workers and the workplace. Sometimes simply seeing what work is and how it's done can be revelatory. Twenty years ago, the Ms. Foundation launched the Take Our Daughters to Work program to give girls a close-up look at careers they might never have known about or dreamt of choosing. In a sense, the photographs that Sara Macel made for this book—sometimes charming, often sly, always heartfelt—allowed her to do something similar; in them, she considers her father's career, but from the more nuanced vantage point of adulthood and with a daughter's loving, and an artist's critical, eye.

As a child, Macel had a limited understanding of what her father did after he drove off and traveled far away to work. A few years ago when Dennis Macel, a telephone pole salesman, began talking about phasing out of his long and successful career, his daughter sensed the time was right to learn more about him. Instead of tagging along or shadowing her father on sales trips, Macel devised an ingenious conceptual approach to accomplish that. Instead of dutifully recording the details of a road trip, she's created a meditation on one. *May the Road Rise to Meet You* was designed as, and quickly became, a collaborative and performative project in which father and daughter would learn things about each other and themselves.

The photographs, at first glance, seem straightforward. But they are not. Macel's lovely color palette, skillful handling of light, and assured sense of composition all work together to infuse the images with a palpable sense of place and nostalgia. Her interest in ambiguity and nuance gives this shrewd, ambitious project its edge and lifts it to an unexpectedly emotional and complex plane. After forty-four years on the road, Dennis Macel estimates he's been away from home more than 4,000 days, traveled close to 8 million miles, and sold 36,000 telephone poles a year. The challenge to his daughter was to figure out—in retrospect and through roughly forty images—how to respond to and represent all of that and then even more.

Macel's solution was to consider options and make images along a road that not only stretched from place to place, but from present to past and from fact to fiction. She made pictures on the road trips she took with her father, then set off on her own without him. She made pictures about what he actually did, then conceived of and produced images about what she imagined he might have done. Presented here, those images speak to the ways that photographers and photographs can tell stories and play games with memory. This book, ostensibly about one man, turns out to be about men in general, about men as seen by women, about parents as seen by their children. Photographs of Dennis Macel—depicted behind the steering wheels of big cars or sitting on the edge of hotel beds with a remote control or drink in hand—evoke thoughts about adventure, loneliness, communication, masculinity, family, nature, capitalism. And they remind us how photography plays a central role in defining them all.

The utility poles that make costarring or cameo appearances in these photographs are, as quick research reveals, durable products because they are thoroughly soaked in wood preservatives. And one could argue that Macel's photographs are similarly reinforced by the photographic history that has, willfully or indirectly, been infused into them. They draw strength from a legacy that stretches from Darius Kinsey's nineteenth-century, glass-plate images of logging in the Pacific Northwest to the touching portraits Larry Sultan made of his father—*Pictures from Home* (1982–91)—that show a dispirited man who put up a brave front in his forced retirement. Macel's road pictures acknowledge the lure of the road and iconic pictures of it made by Dorothea Lange in the 1930s, Robert Frank in the 1950s, and Robert Adams twenty years after that. The work nods to Stephen Shore's photographs from the early 1970s, stately color images of mundane intersections and moments, and to Mitch Epstein's elegiac *Family Business* (2003), an end-of-an-era examination of the unraveling of his father's furniture business.

What is compelling here, though, isn't Macel's acknowledgment of canonic photographic themes or tropes, but rather the inventive and self-assured way she moves things forward. If traveling salesmen have, over the years, been the butt of jokes and typecast as existential sad sacks, Macel smartly works with and against cultural stereotypes to make sure that her father is not reduced to some stock or archetypical figure. In a mix of images that circle around and stretch notions of what "documentary" is or can mean—some shots are straight as can be, others recreate or reenact—Macel developed an elliptical and remarkably effective storytelling framework.

Because cameras are engineered to indiscriminately vacuum up details of whatever lies in front of them, we expect serious photographers to assert their authorship by staking out a singular subject and stance as they go about their work. What makes Macel's work especially interesting and timely now—as photography is being radically transformed and our relationships to both the medium and reality itself are being reexplored—is the fact that it's hard to say with any certainty who is doing the looking in many of these pictures. In some, we seem to see the world from what is purportedly Dennis Macel's vantage point. In others, we watch him from a distance, as a subject. The intent of some of the photographs seems forthright and purposeful; others seem willfully neutral or evasive. From photograph to photograph perspectives shift, locations turn generic, and time frames start to slip. The images range from objective to subjective and only upon careful examination begin to yield clues to their veracity or meticulous construction. There are establishing shots and close-ups, landscapes and portraits and still lifes. As one might expect, many images have been shot at ground level, but a surprising number were made from above—from airplanes, hotel windows, the tops of staircases—in what feels like an attempt to get some critical distance on her subject. Macel's work, much like the work it depicts, refuses to stand still or settle down.

"May the road rise to meet you" is an old Irish blessing, one meant to reassure with the promise of support over the course of life's unpredictable journey. What's curious about these photographs is that they also hint at another, more unnerving scenario, one in which the open road, a symbol of freedom and the future, transforms itself into the end of a road. In this picture-narrative, we watch a traveling salesman diligently going about his business even as, we suspect, age, online sales, and wireless technology are rewriting the story. As pages turn and Macel's game plan reveals itself, father and daughter—reflecting on their respective careers and time's passing—have devised a way to communicate their mutual love, respect, and vulnerability in photographs whose meanings are far from absolute.

This is not the first story in which photography and utility poles so specifically intersect. Samuel Morse, the American painter and inventor, was in Paris in 1839 when the world's frenzied fascination with photography began. He returned to the States to practice photography, spread word of the new medium, and install the first above-ground wooden poles that supported the wires carrying early telegraphic messages along the road from Washington to Baltimore. Then, as now, images, information, and industry are spread by movement. And as Macel's work powerfully reminds us, we continue to make and marvel at photographs as, inevitably, they rise up to comfort us from one moment to another and along the road of life from one generation to the next.

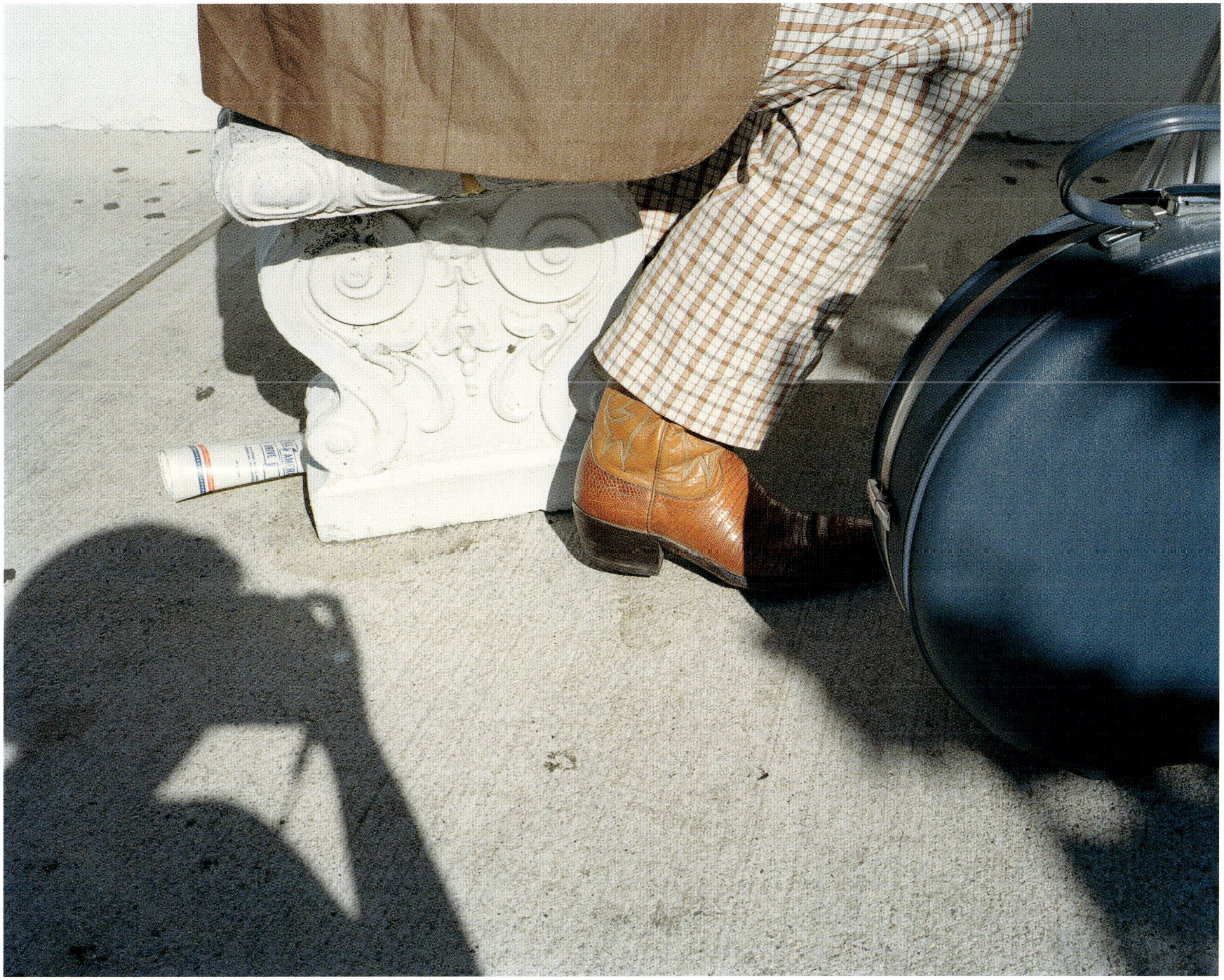

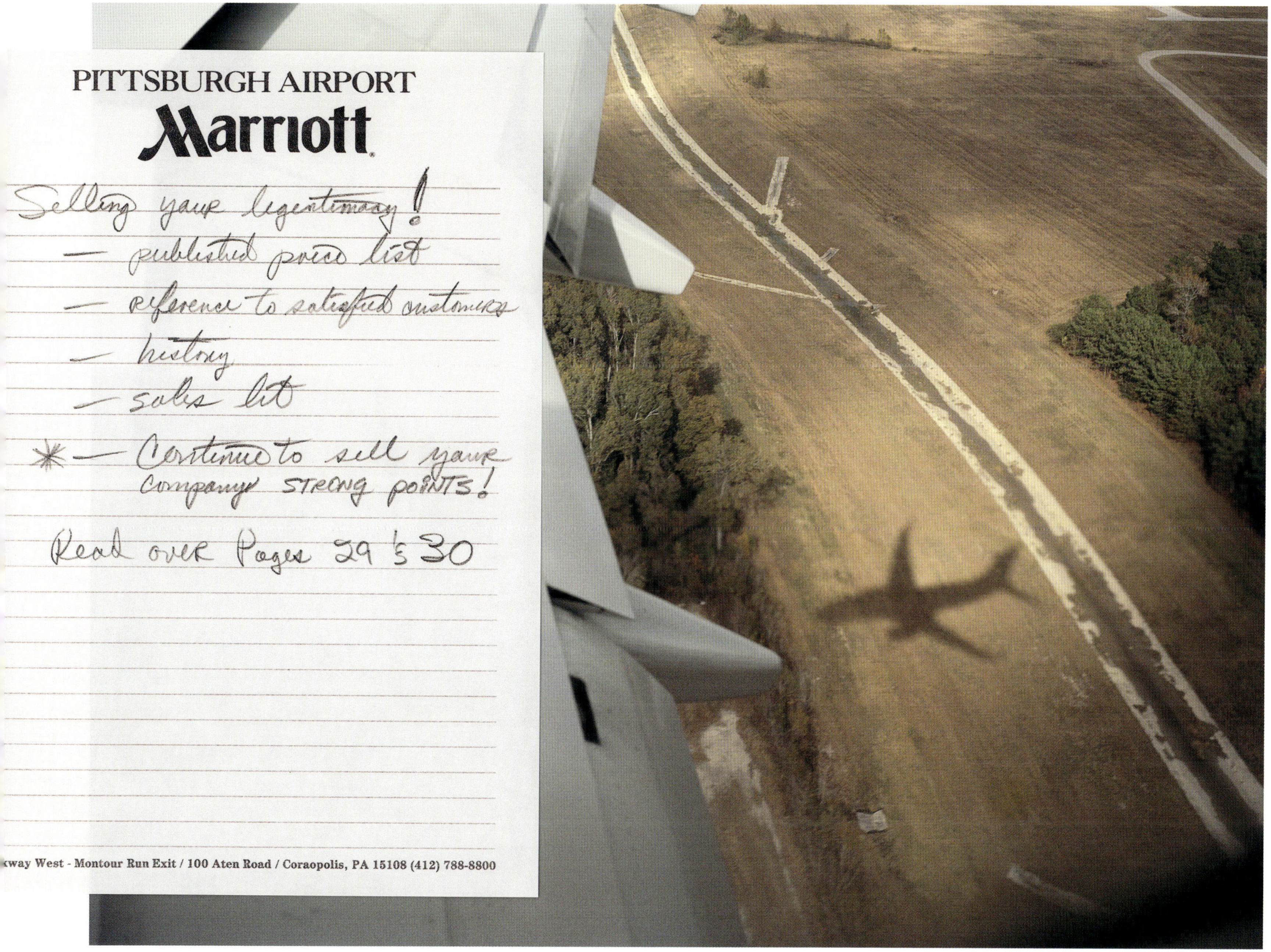
PITTSBURGH AIRPORT
Marriott
Selling your legentimacy!
— published price list
— reference to satisfied customers
— history
— sales lit
*— Continue to sell your company's STRONG POINTS!
Read over Pages 29 & 30
kway West - Montour Run Exit / 100 Aten Road / Coraopolis, PA 15108 (412) 788-8800

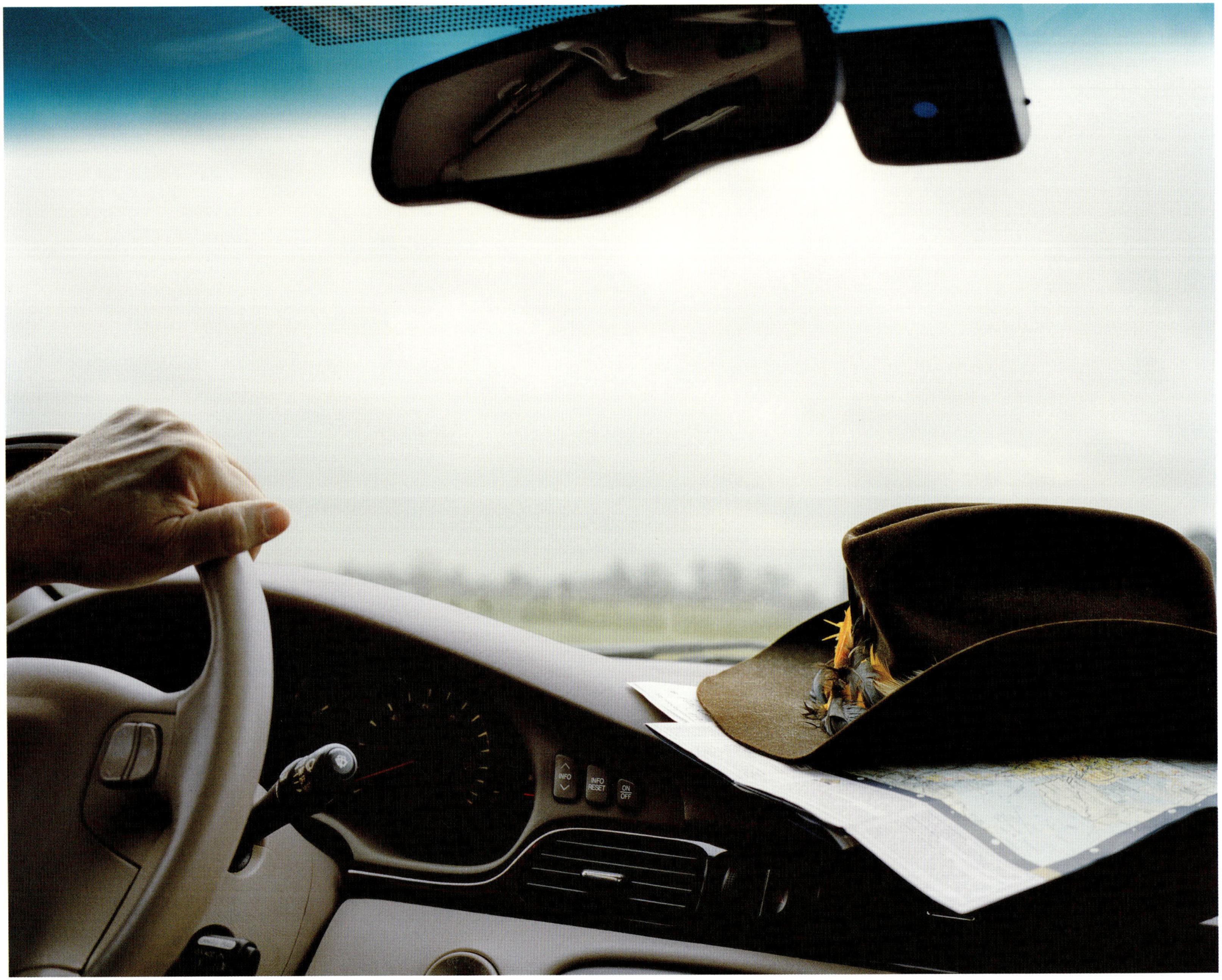
INFO
INFO RESET
ON OFF

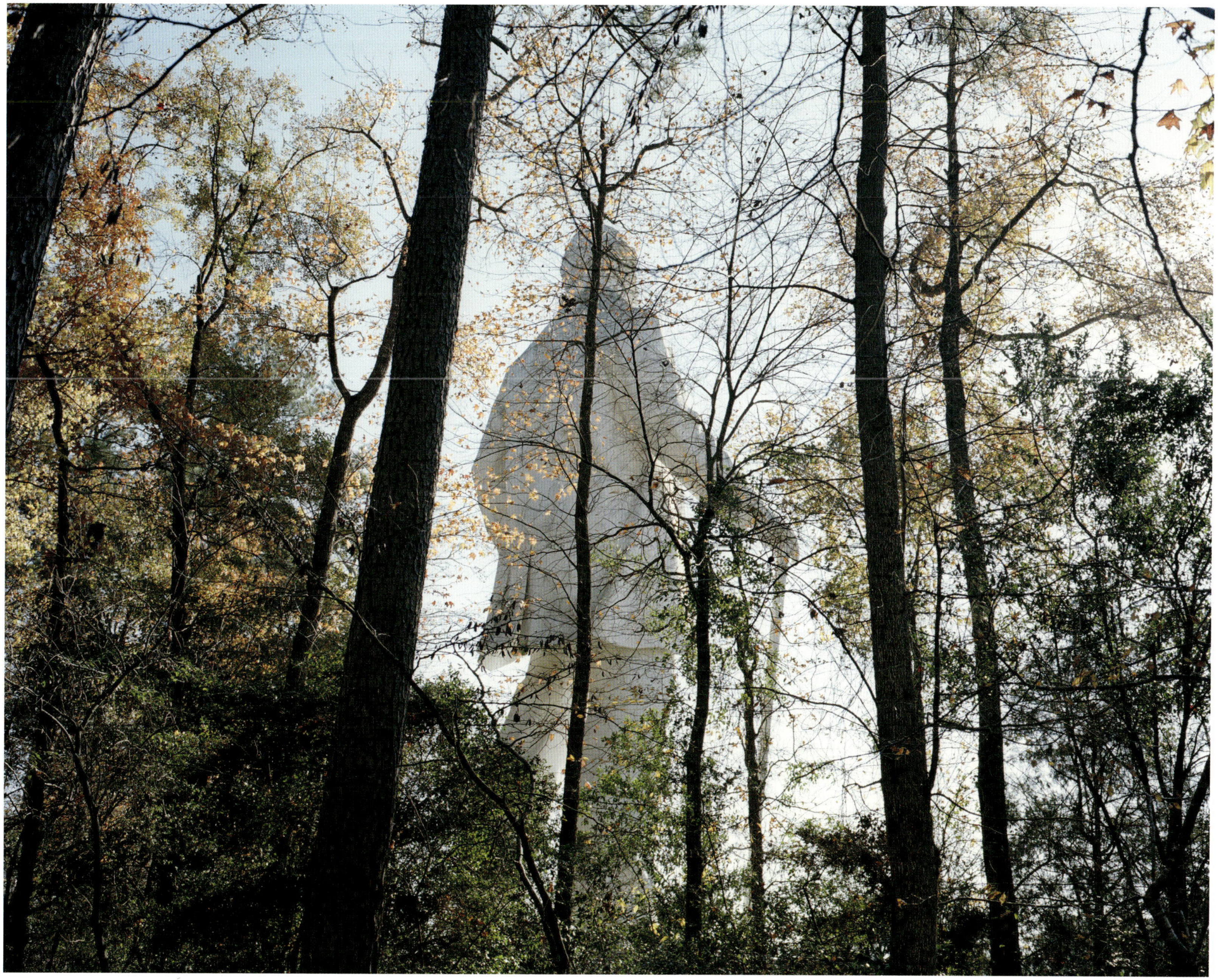

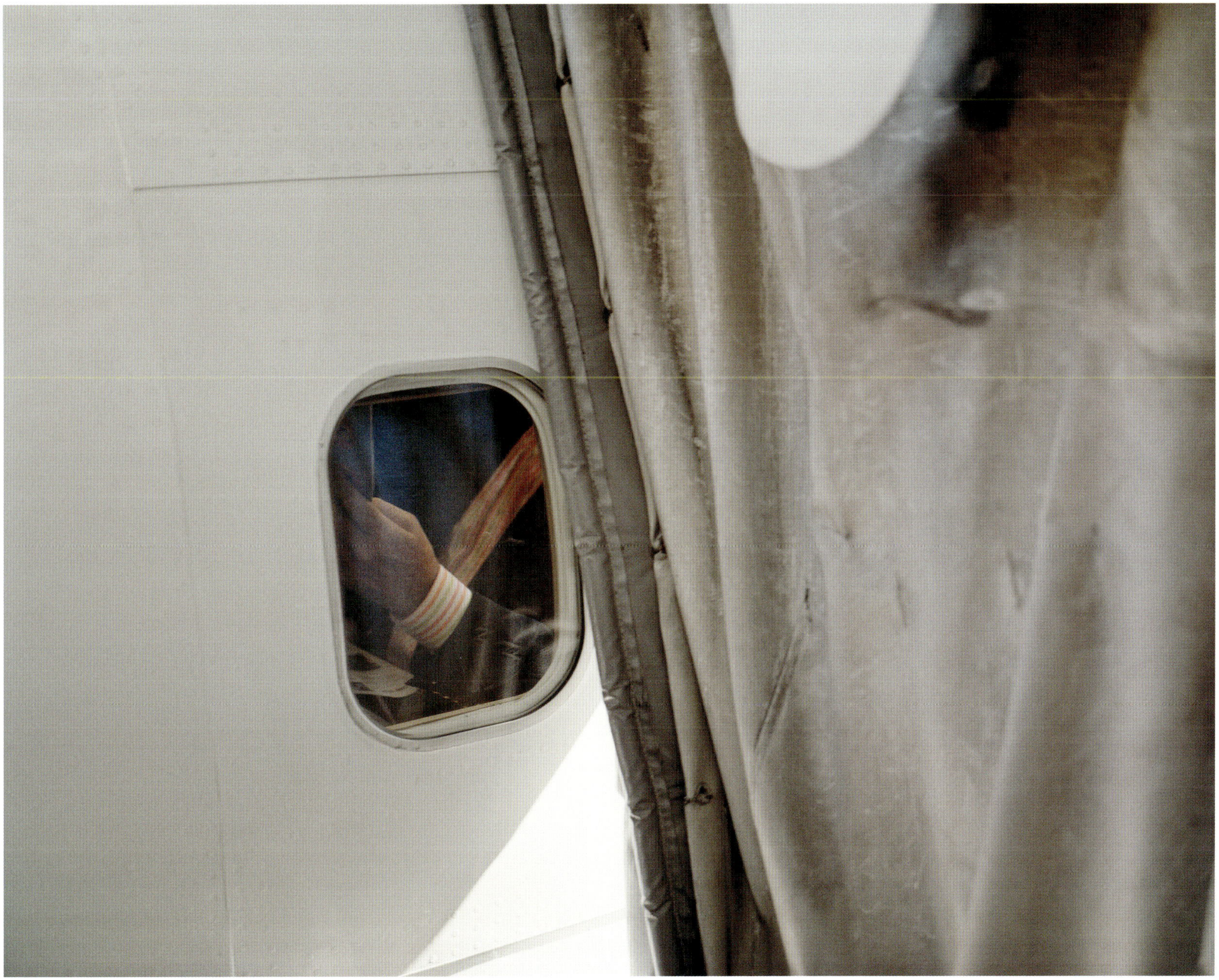

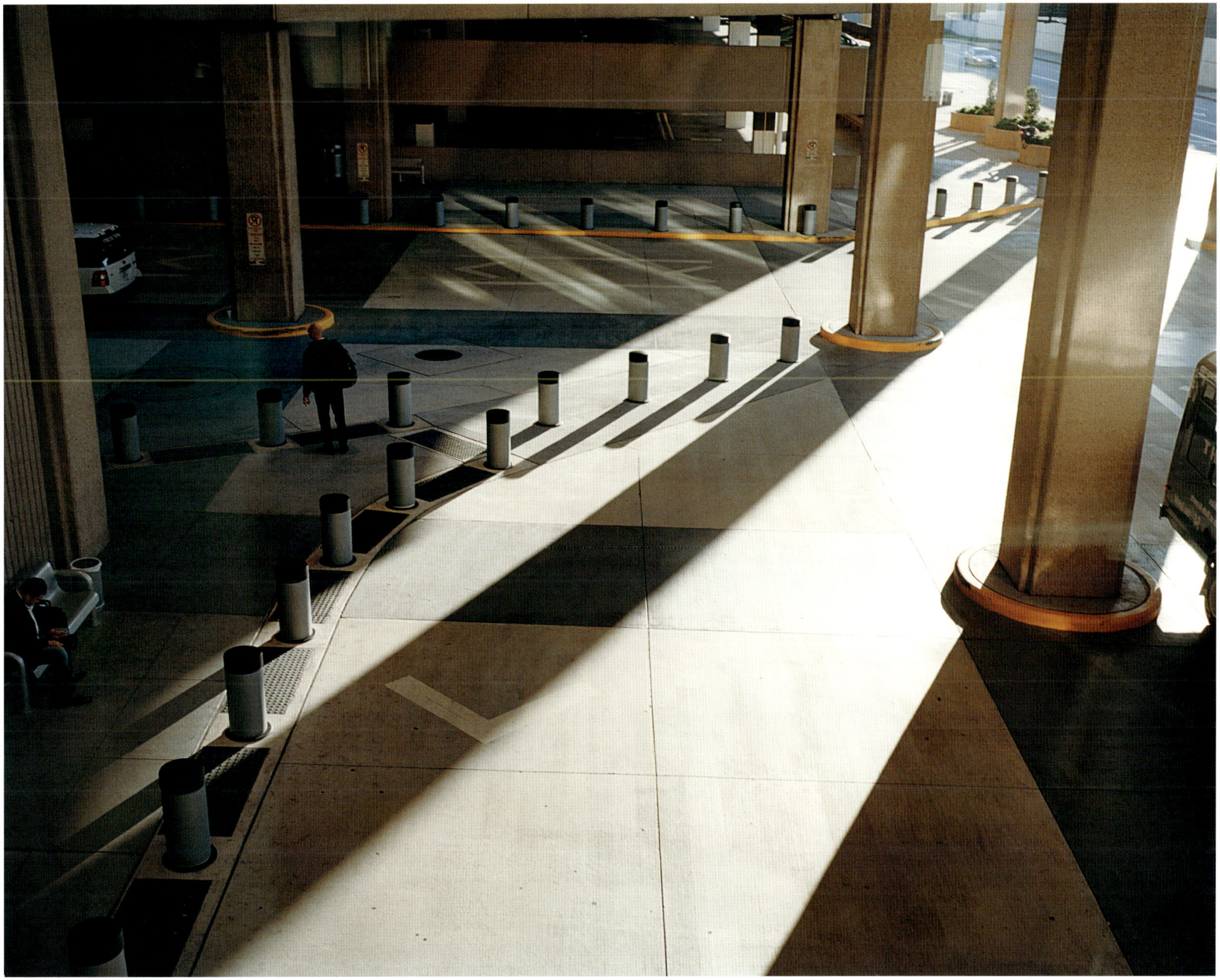

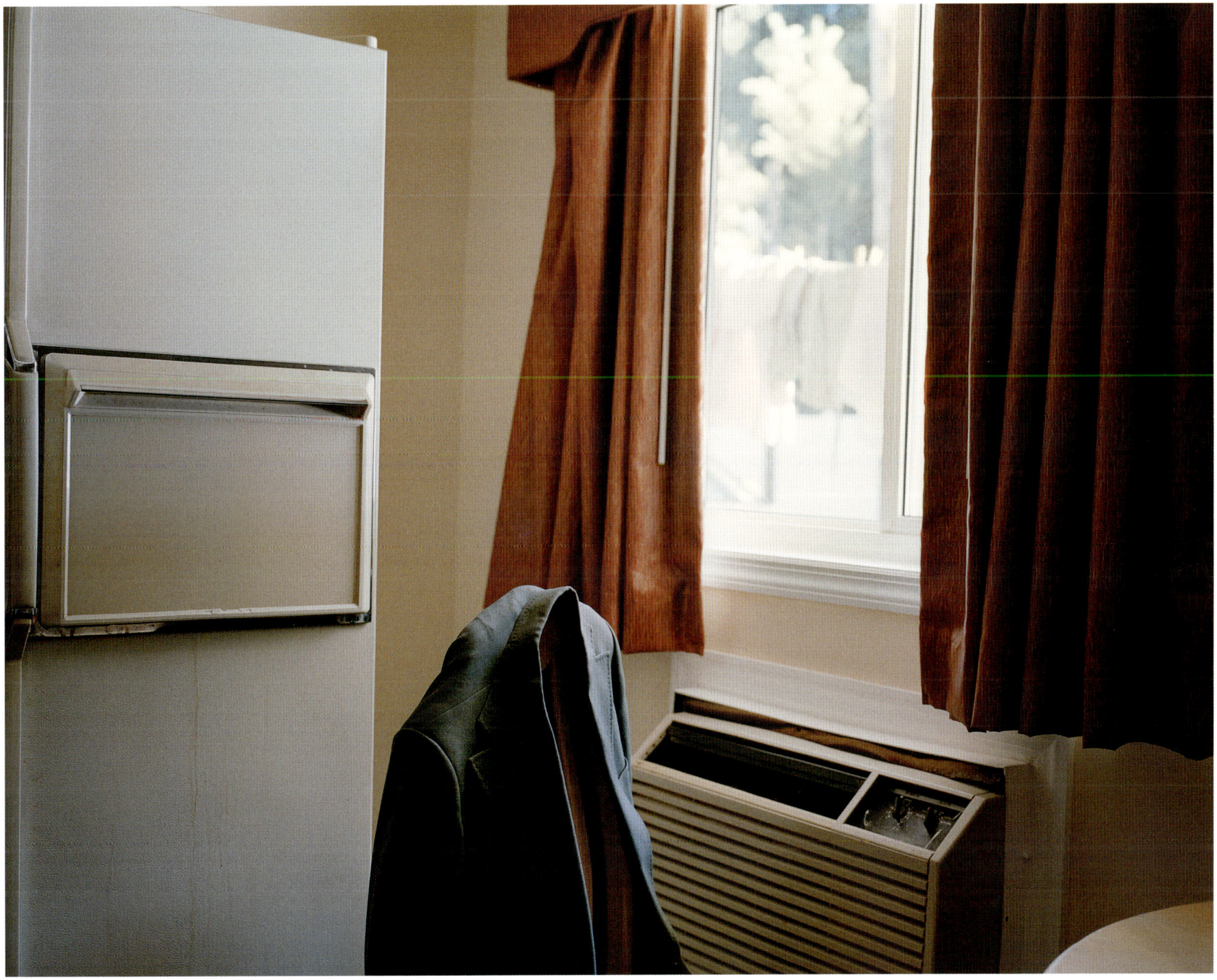

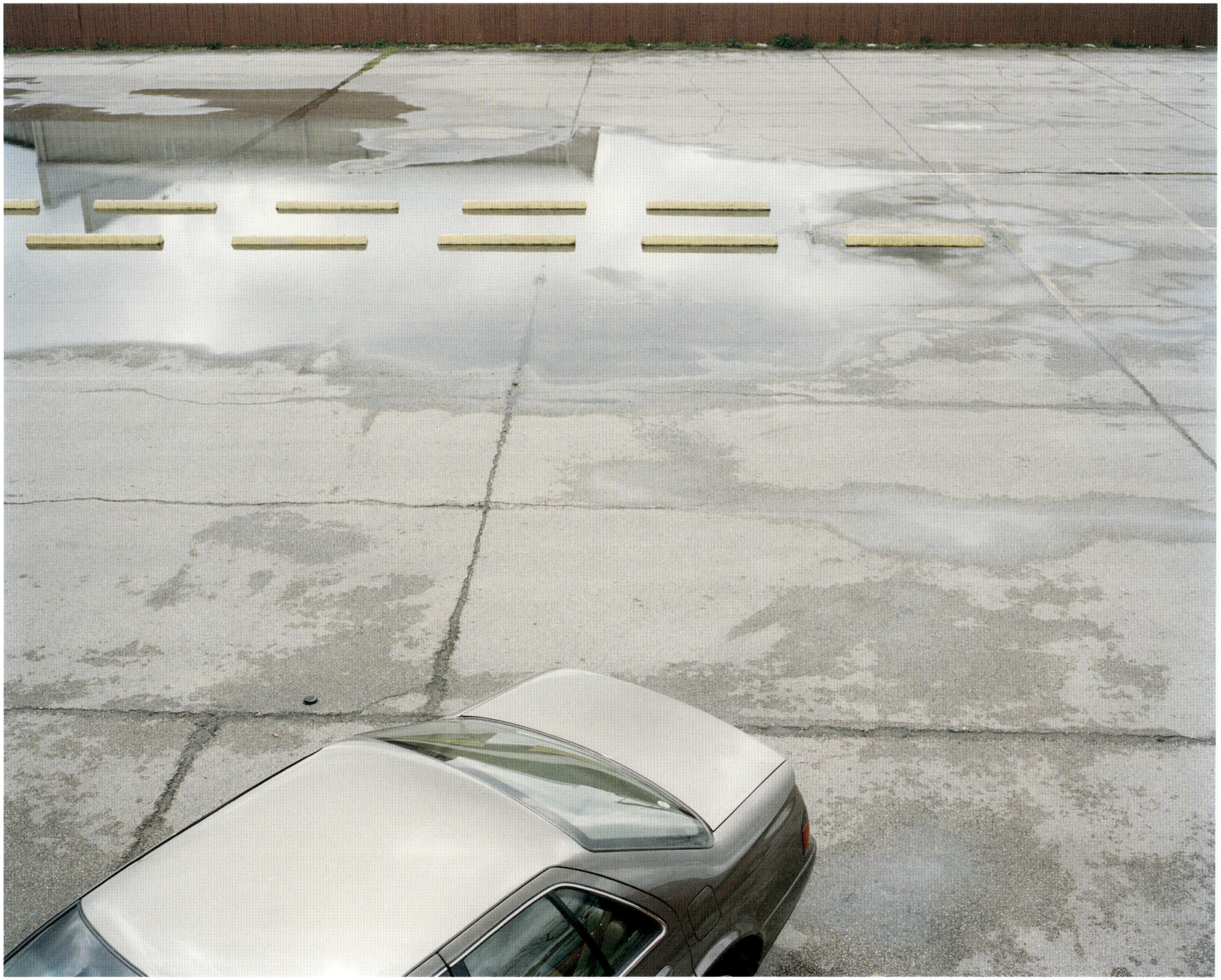

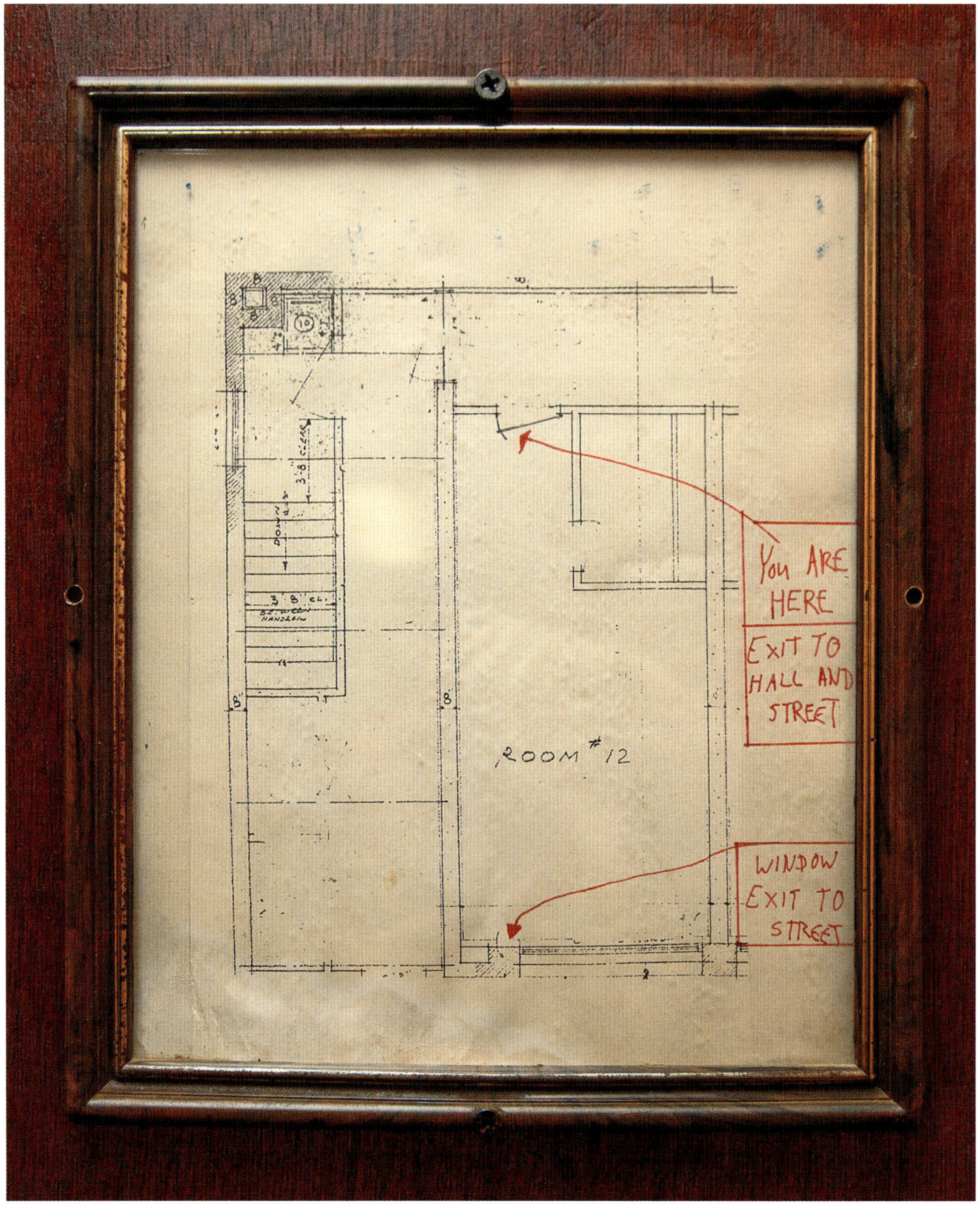
YOU ARE HERE
EXIT TO HALL AND STREET
ROOM #12
WINDOW EXIT TO STREET

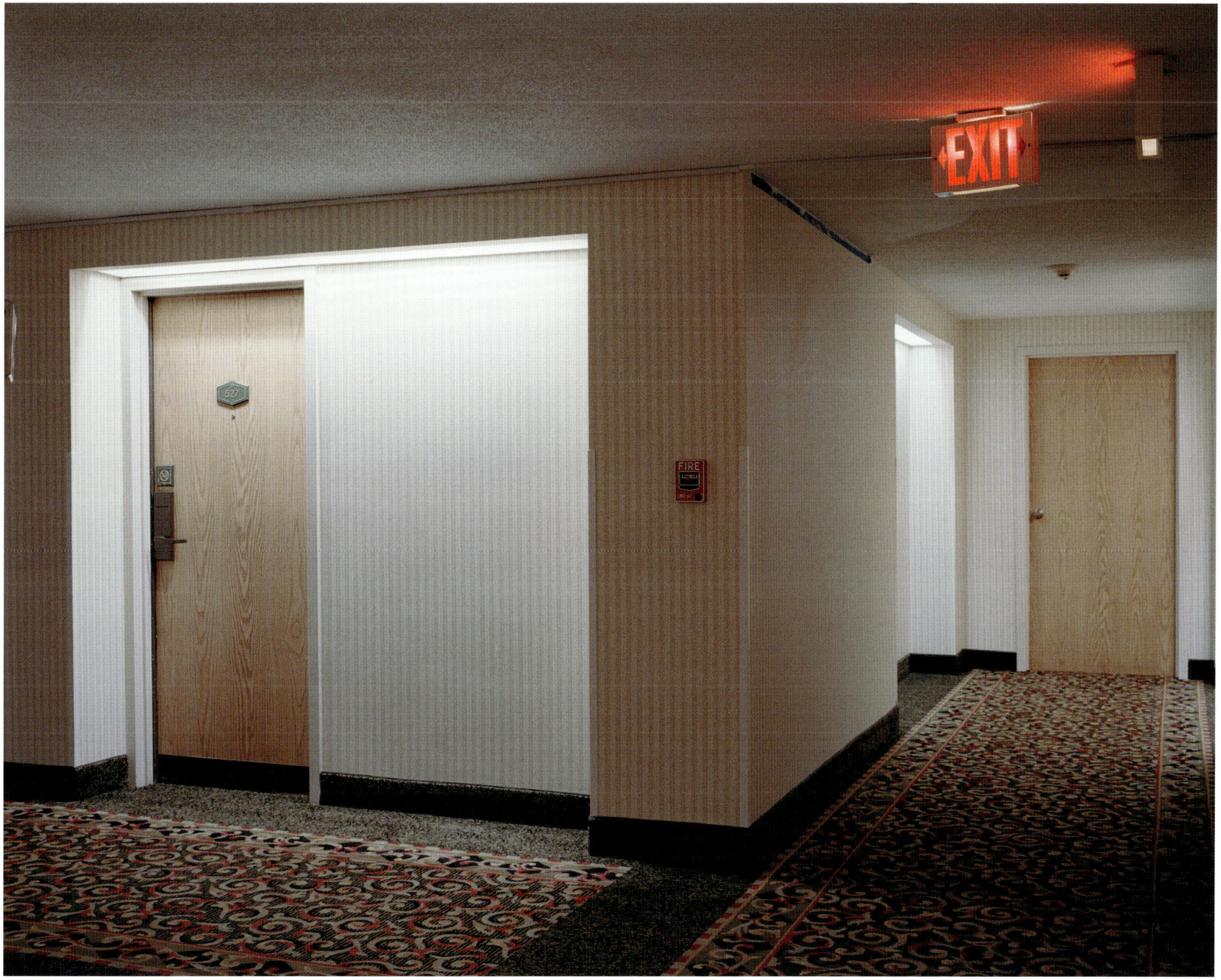
EXIT
527
FIRE

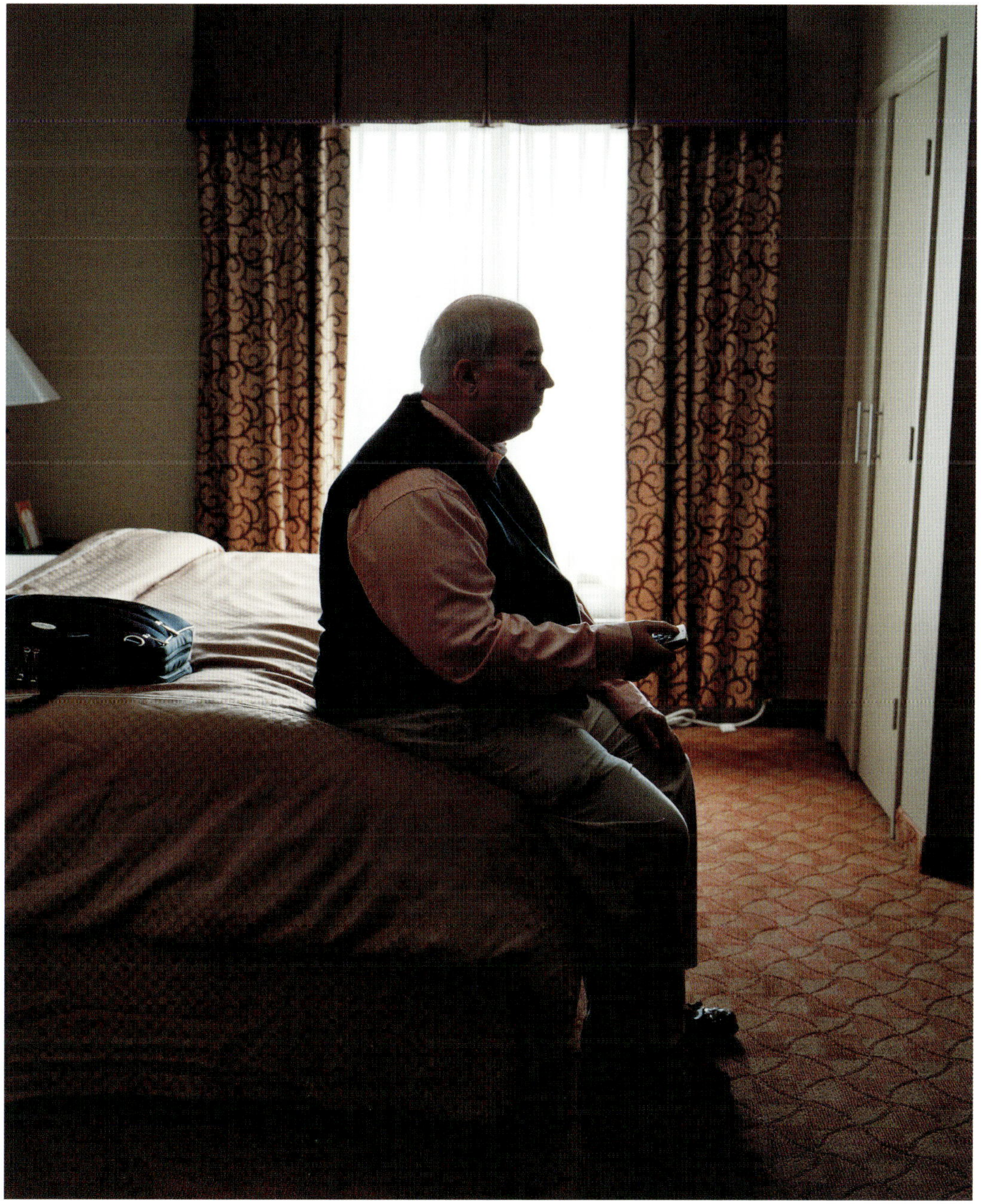

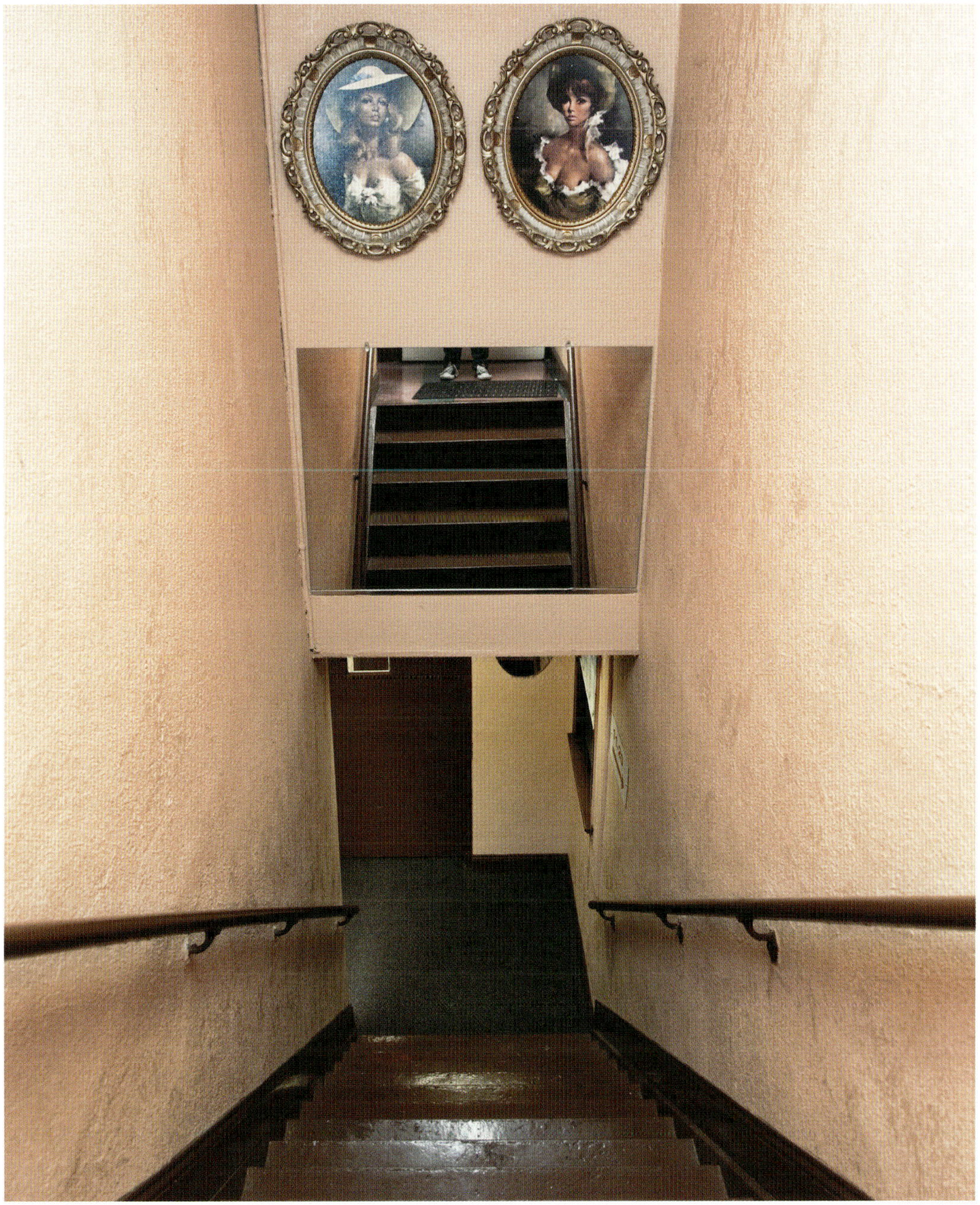

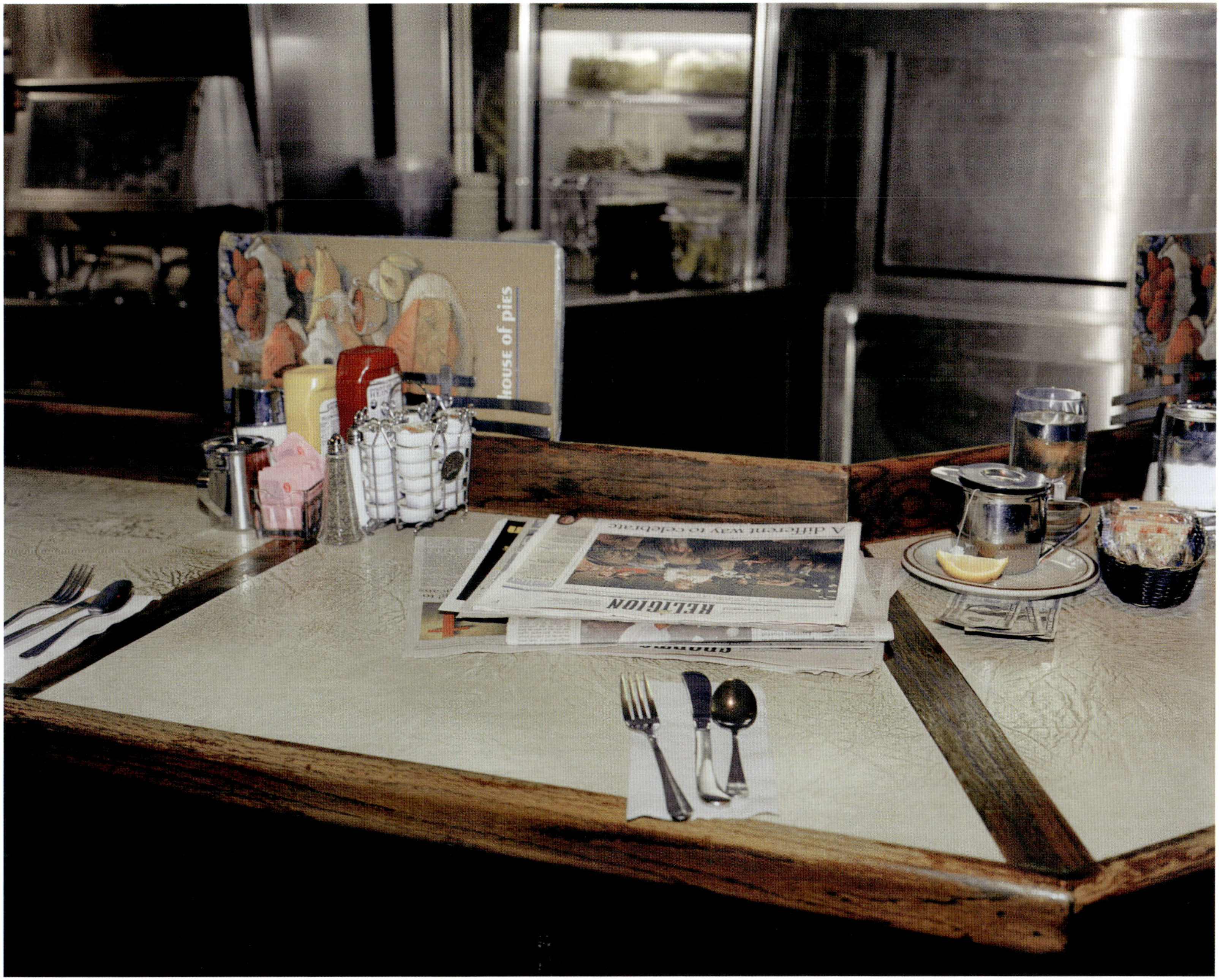
house of pies

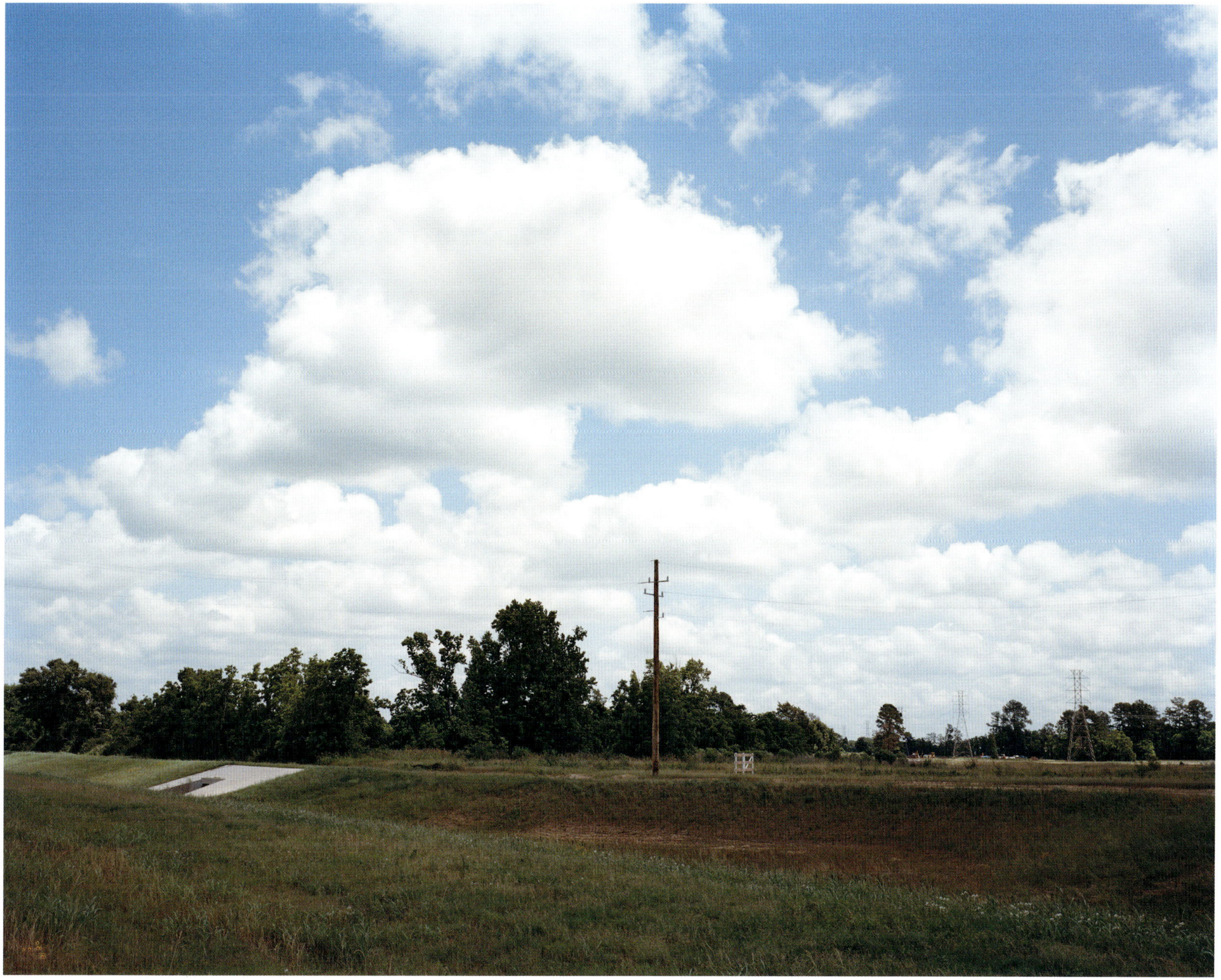

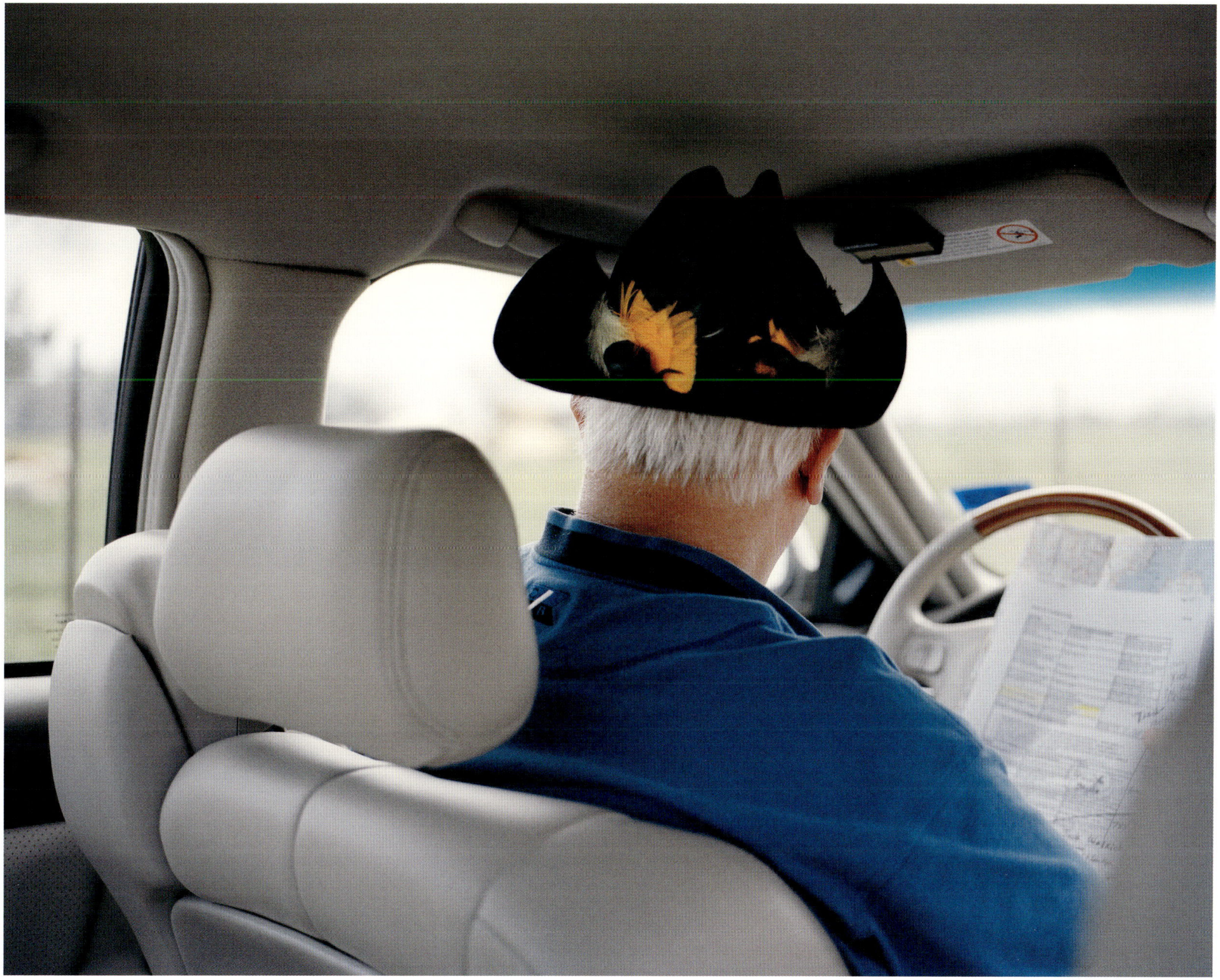

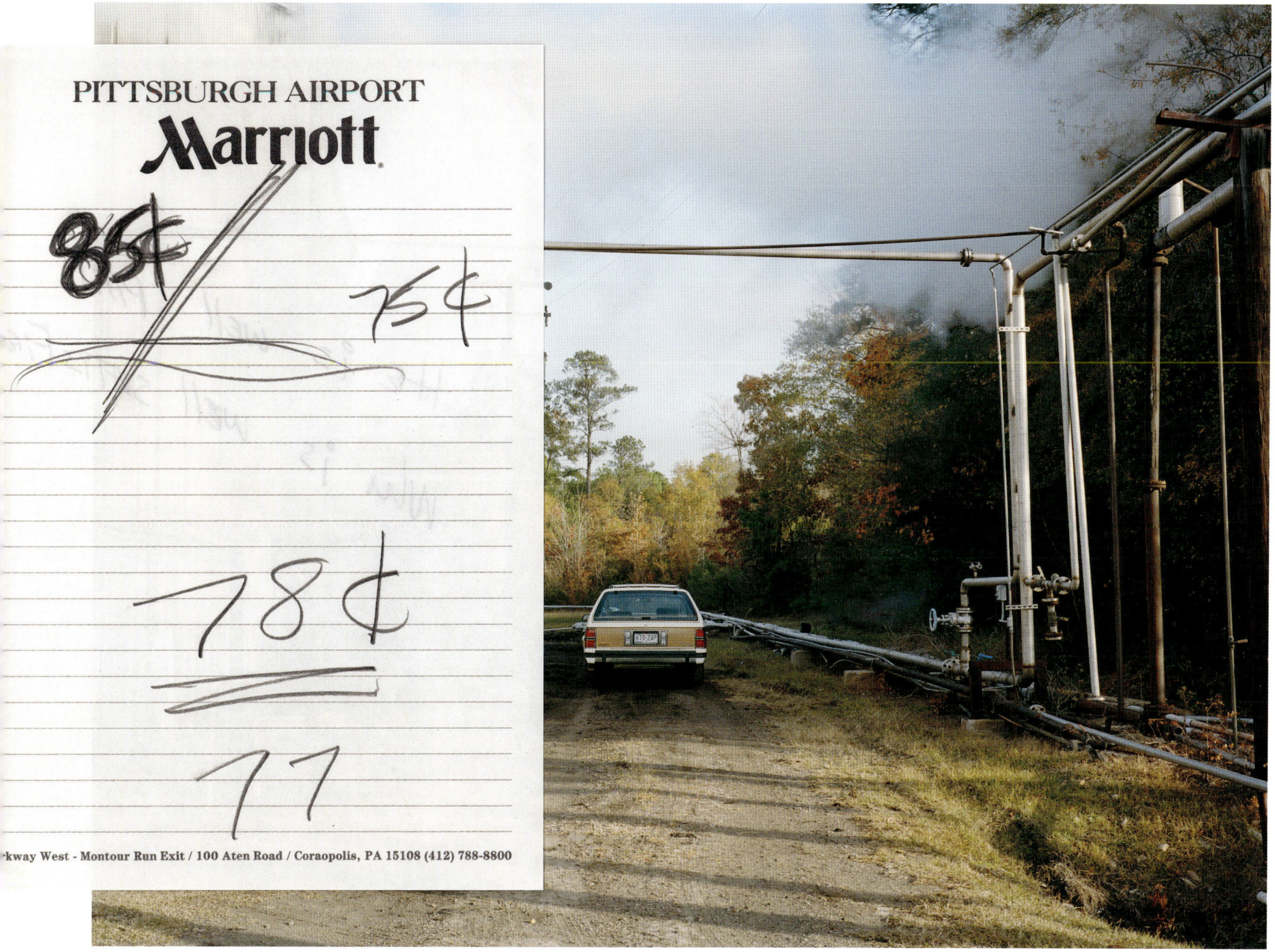
PITTSBURGH AIRPORT
Marriott
85¢
75¢
78¢
77
kway West - Montour Run Exit / 100 Aten Road / Coraopolis, PA 15108 (412) 788-8800

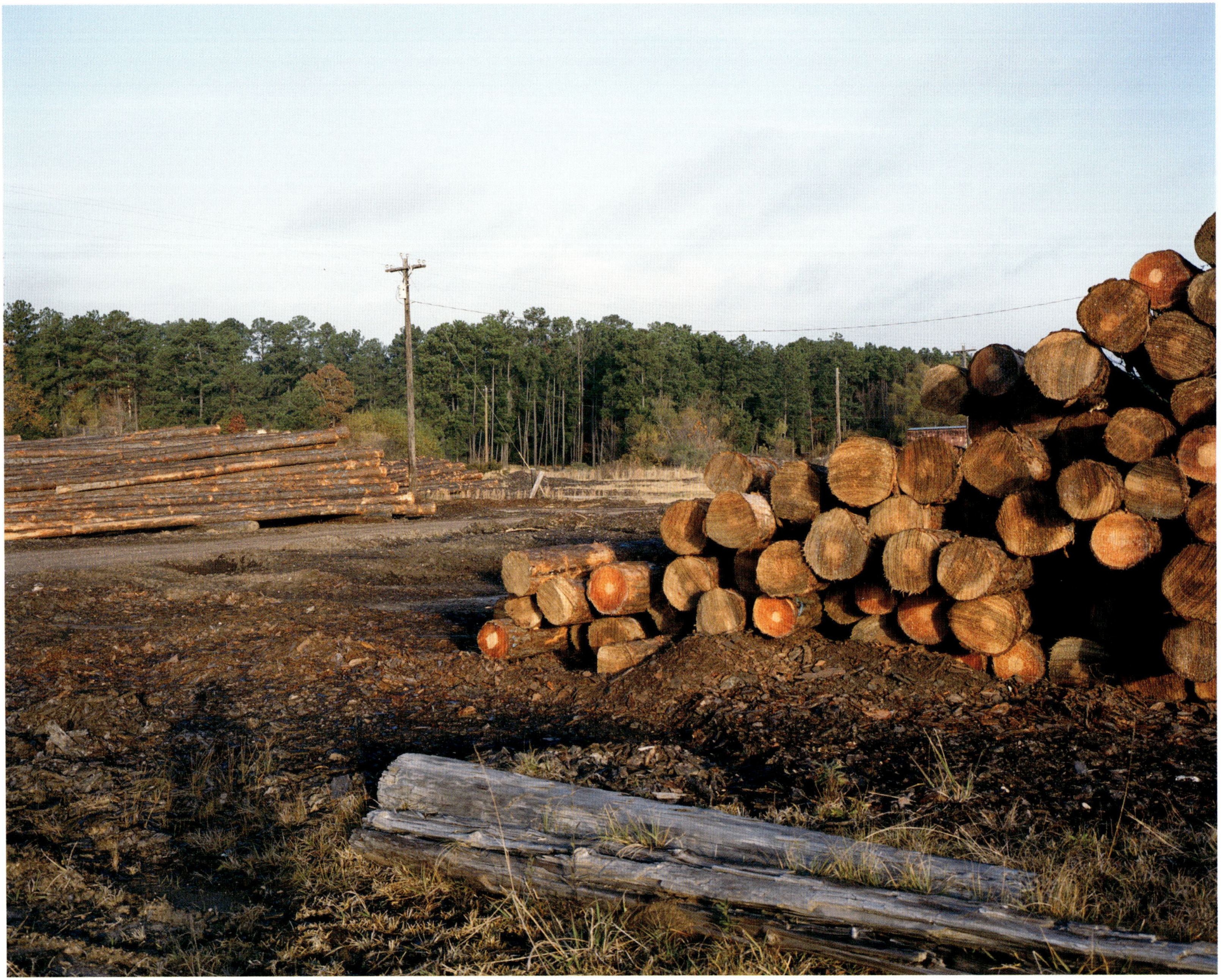

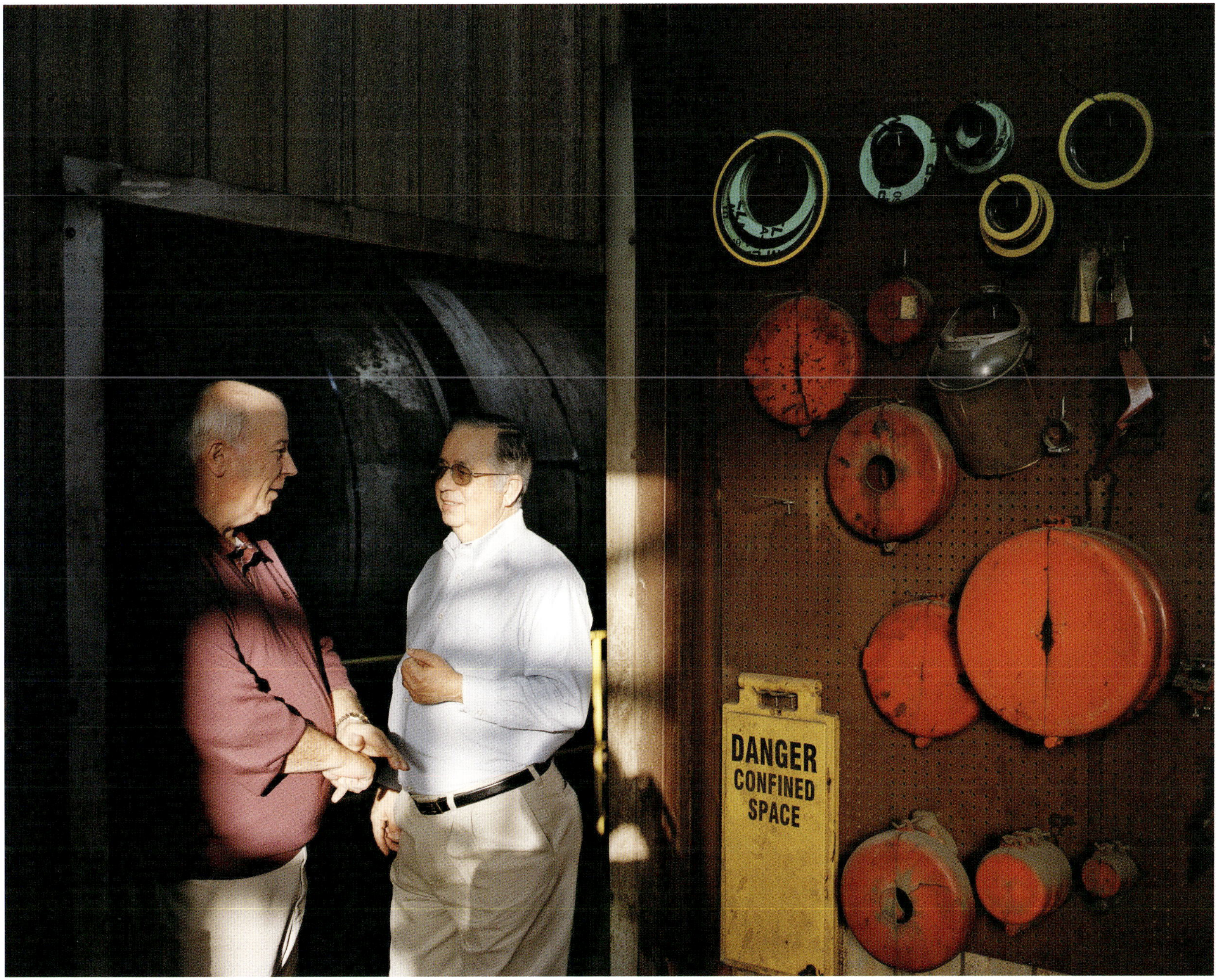
DANGER
CONFINED
SPACE

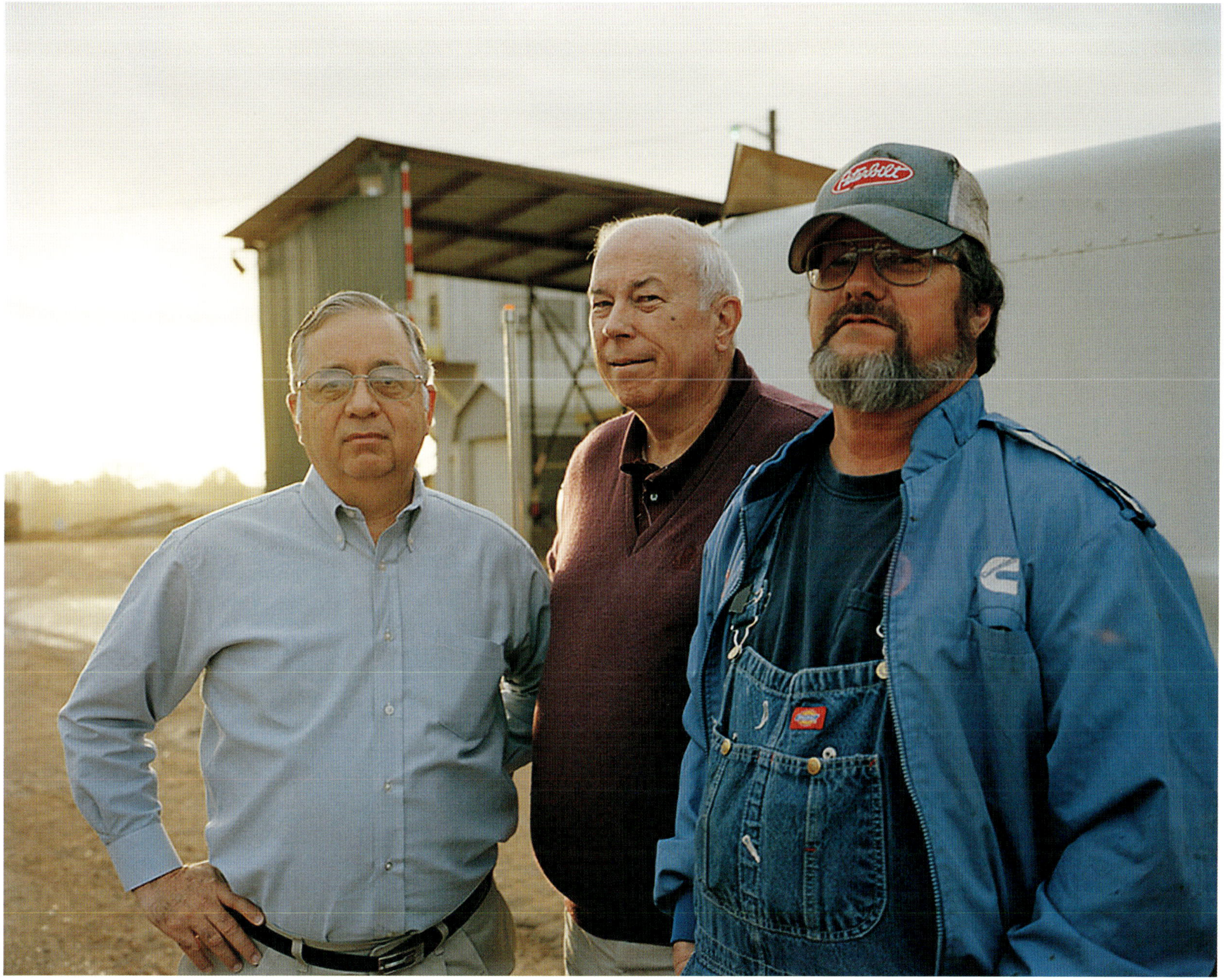

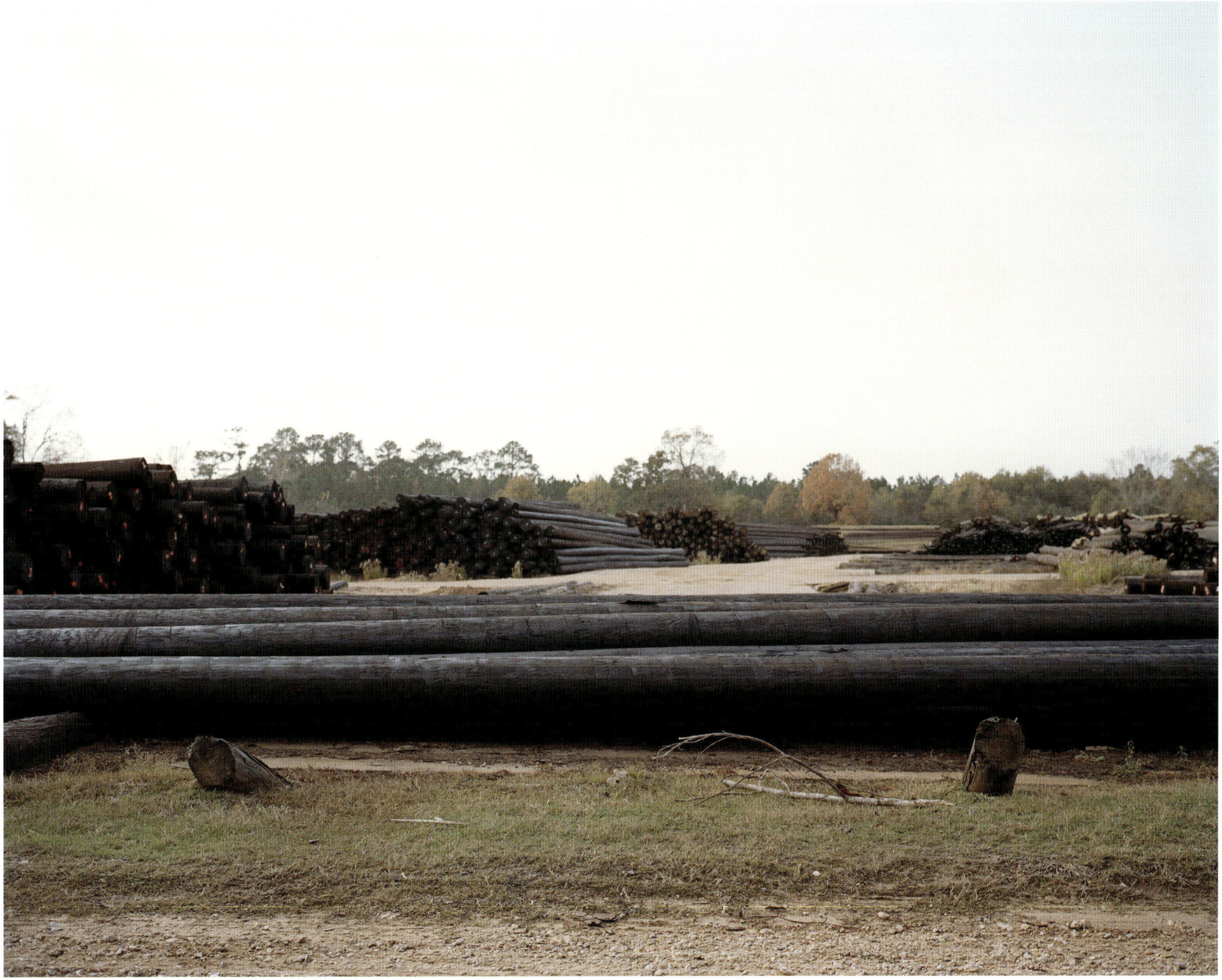

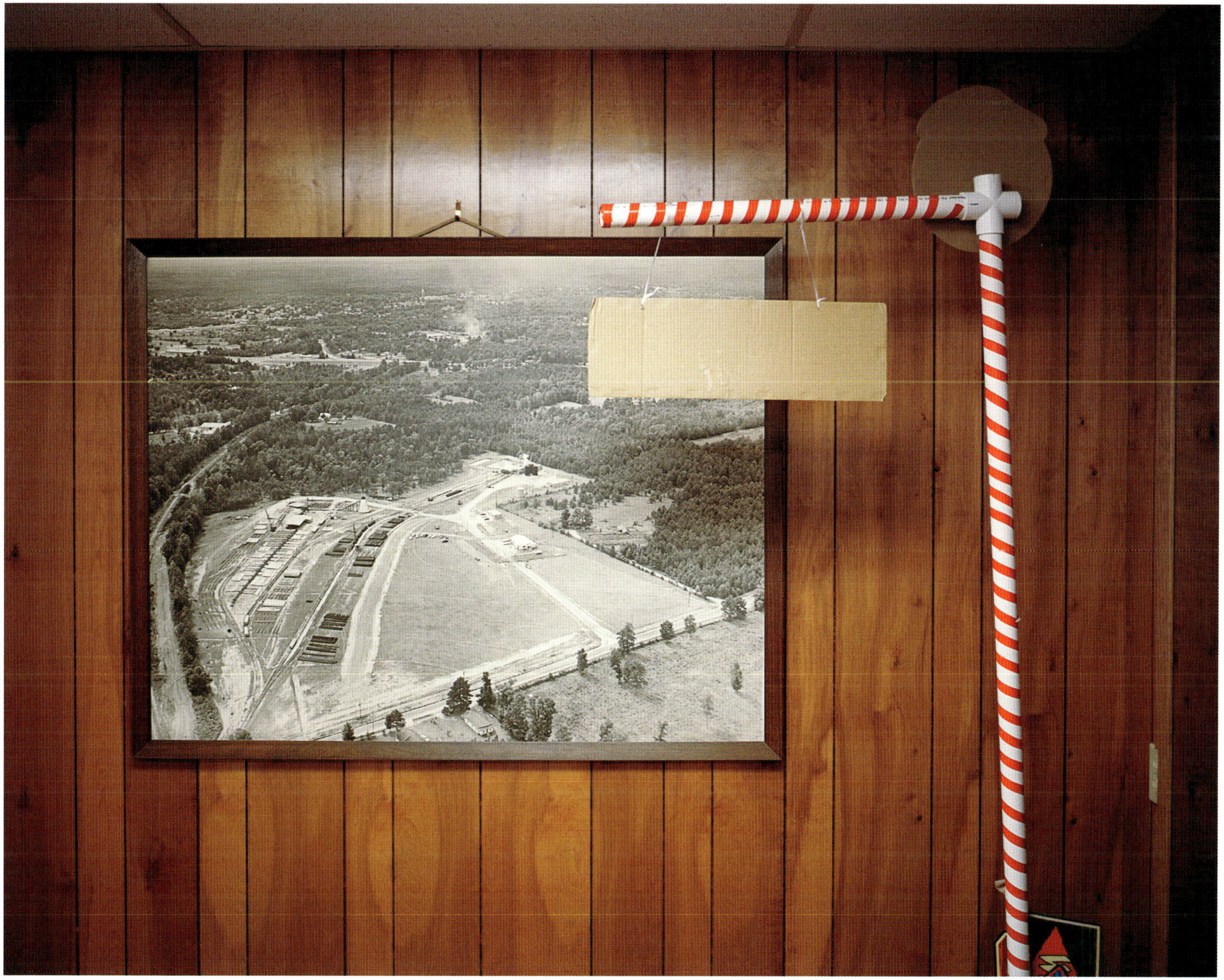

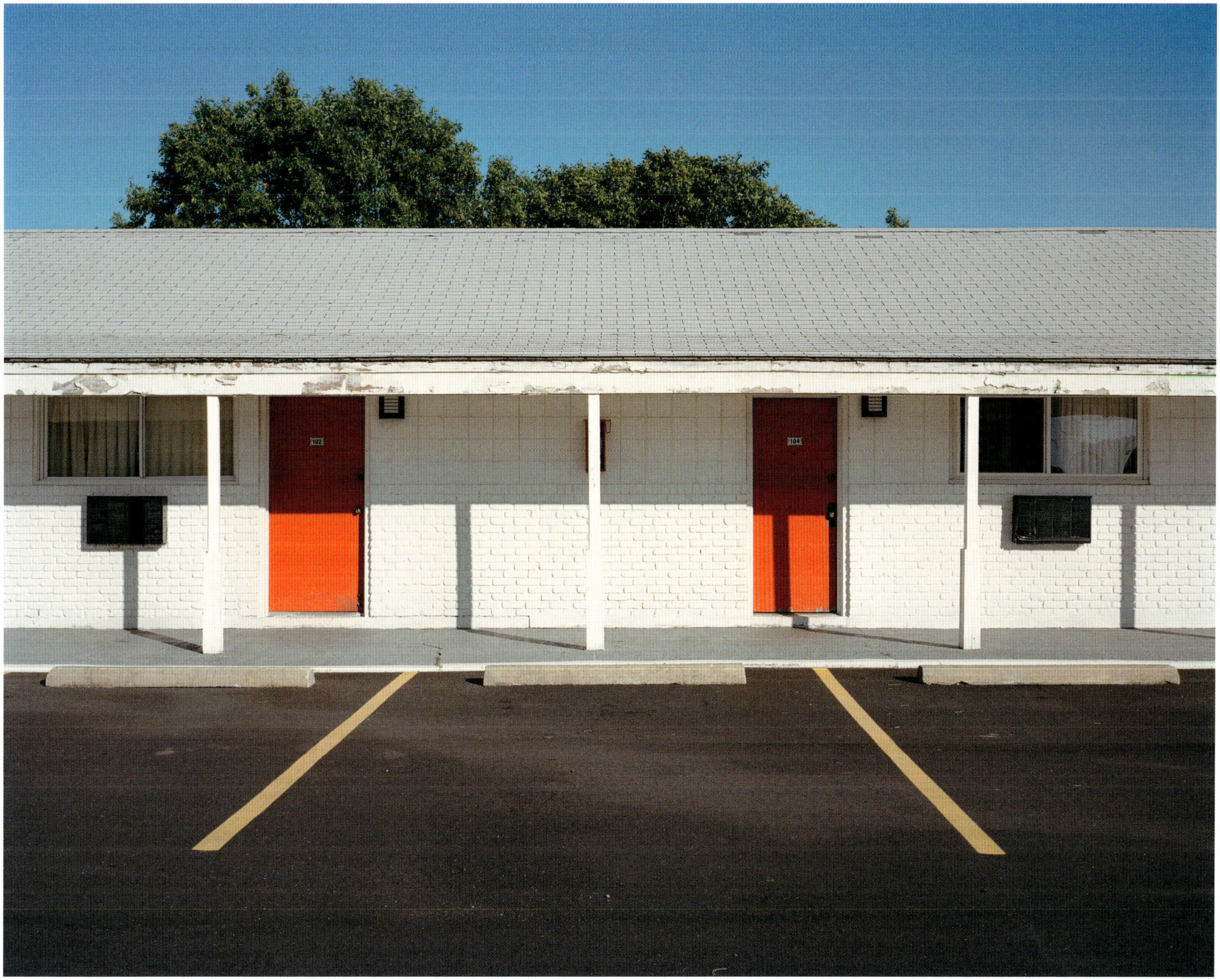
102
104

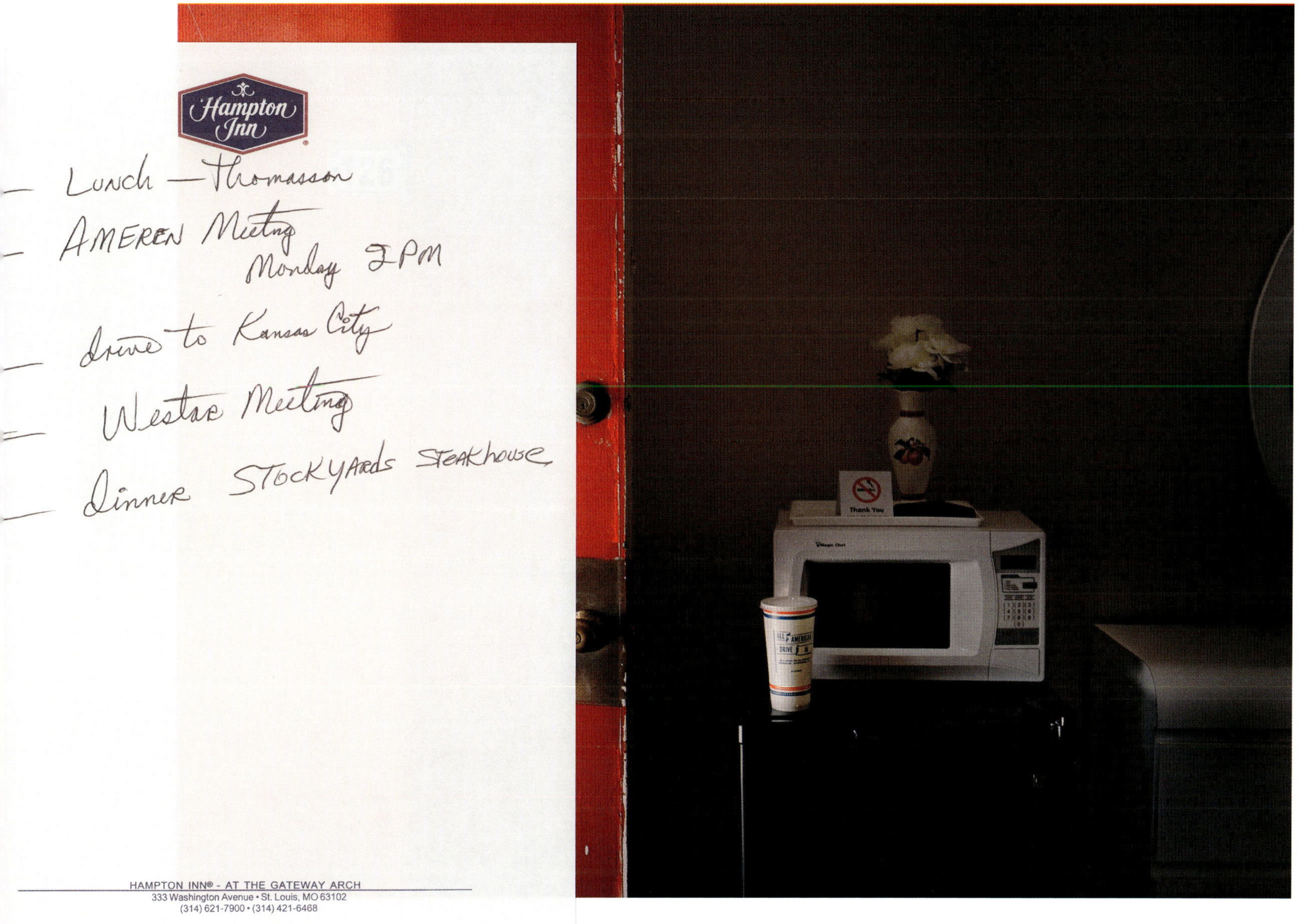
Hampton Inn
Lunch — Thomasson
AMEREN Meeting
Monday 2 PM
Drive to Kansas City
Westar Meeting
Dinner STOCKYARDS STEAKhouse
HAMPTON INN® - AT THE GATEWAY ARCH
333 Washington Avenue • St. Louis, MO 63102
(314) 621-7900 • (314) 421-6468
Thank You

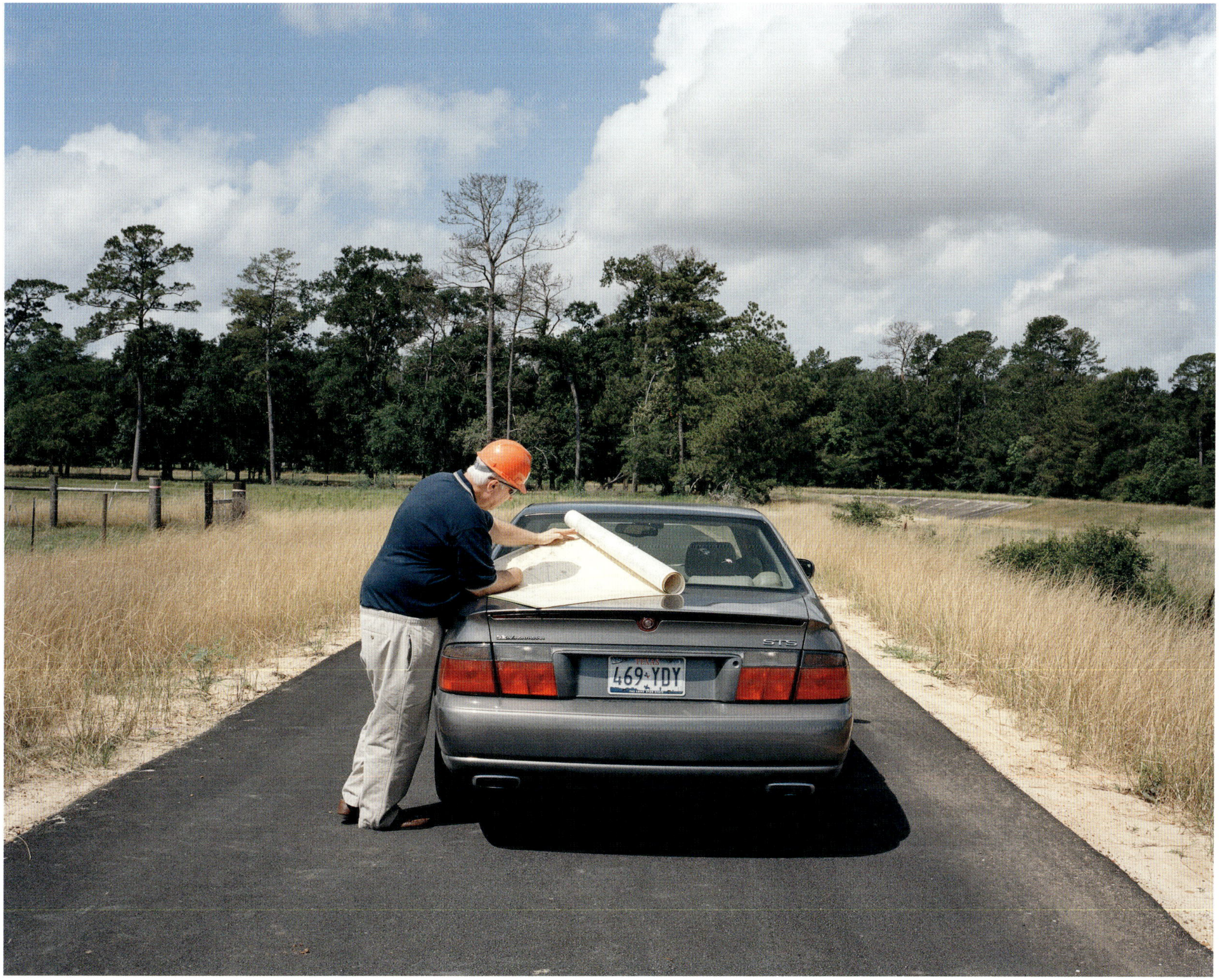
STS
469 YDY

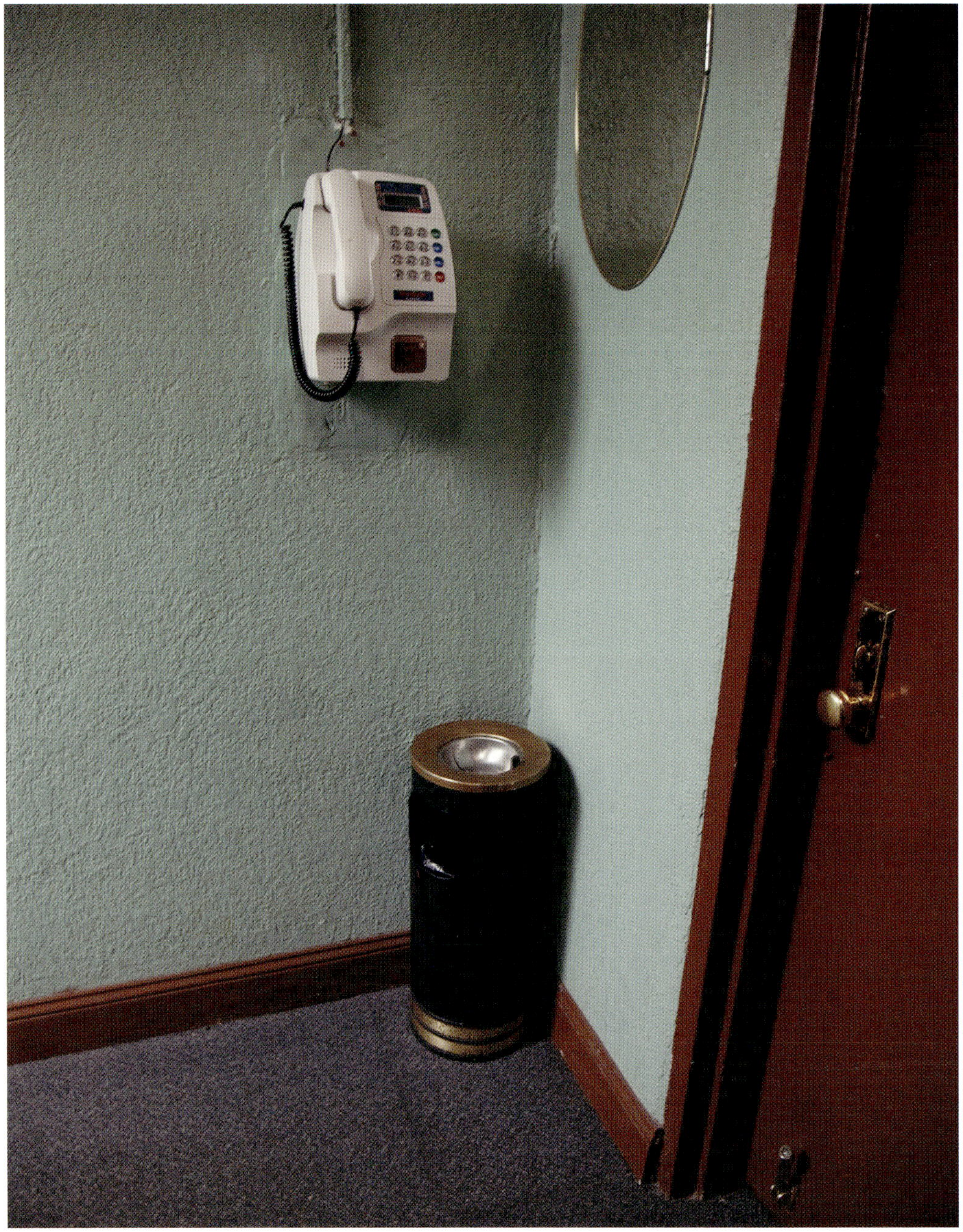

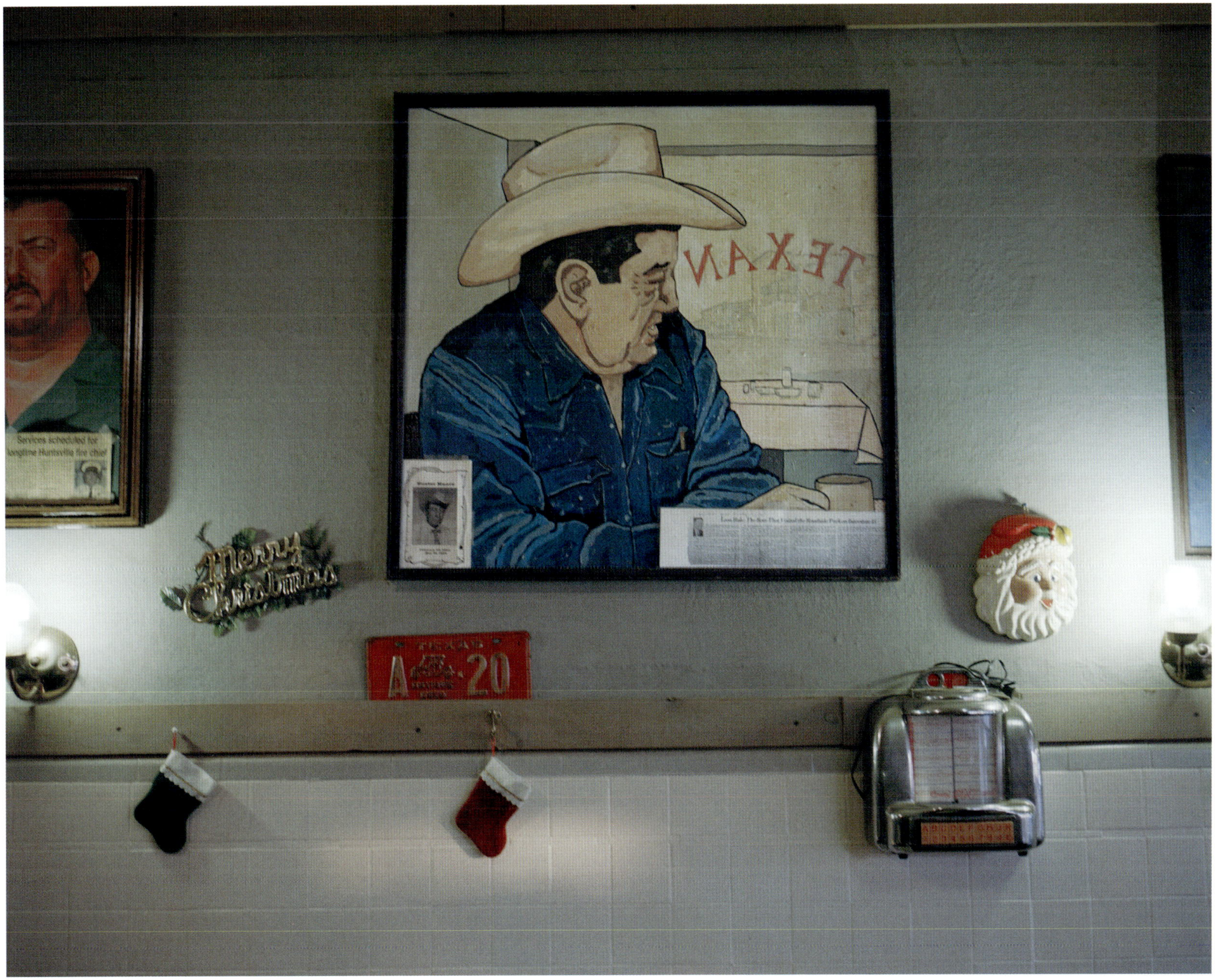
Services scheduled for
longtime Huntsville fire chief
TEXAN
Merry
Christmas
TEXAS
20

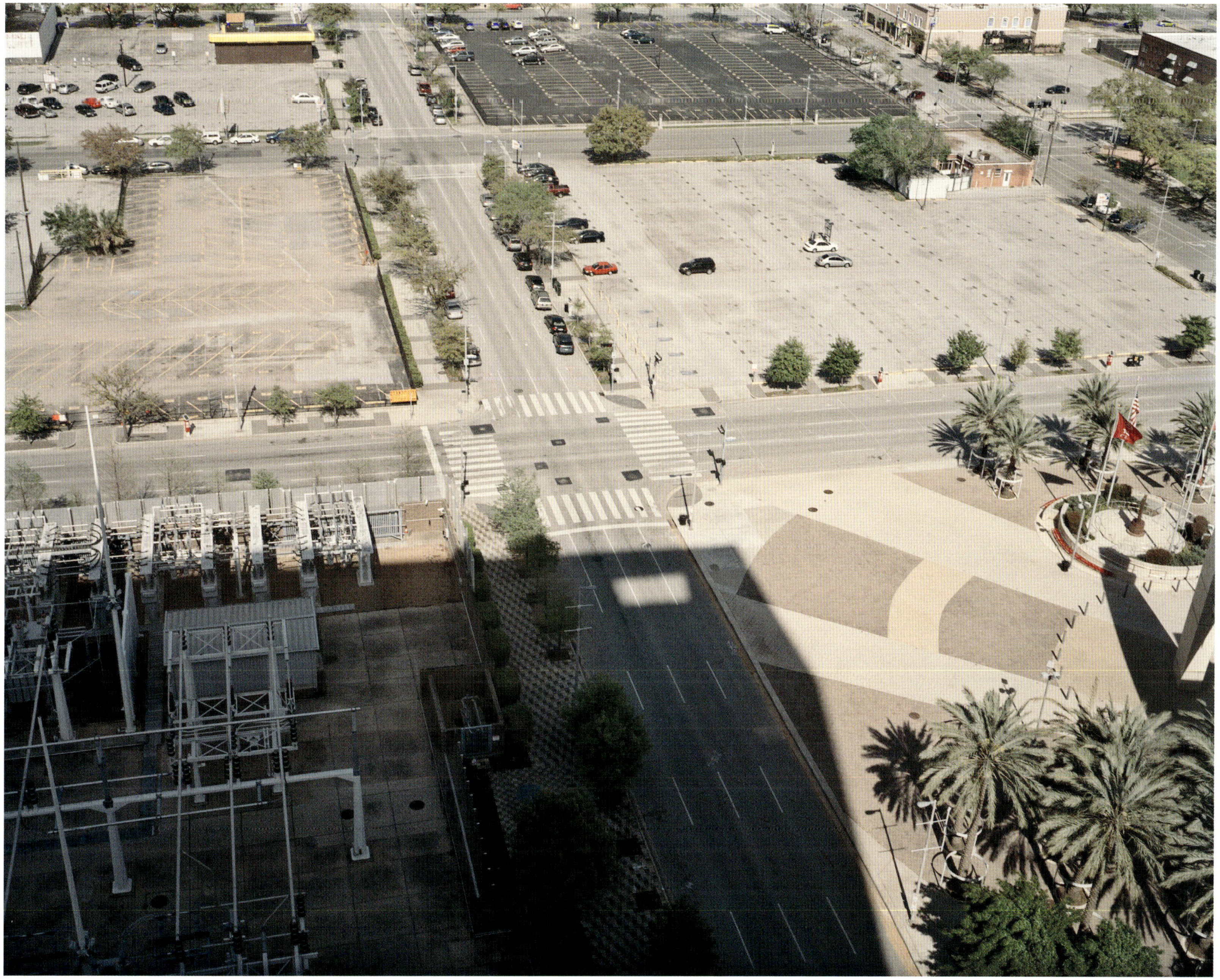

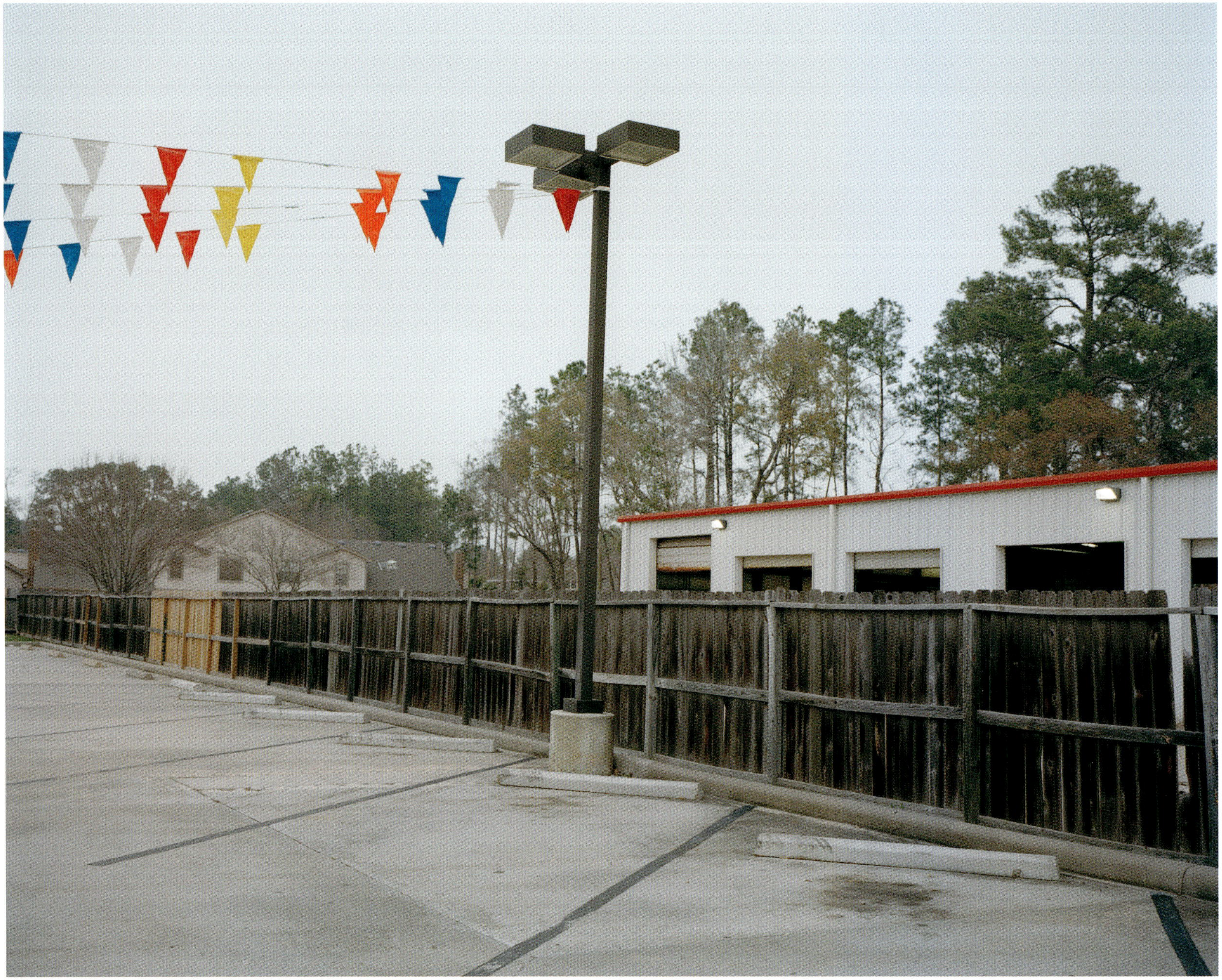

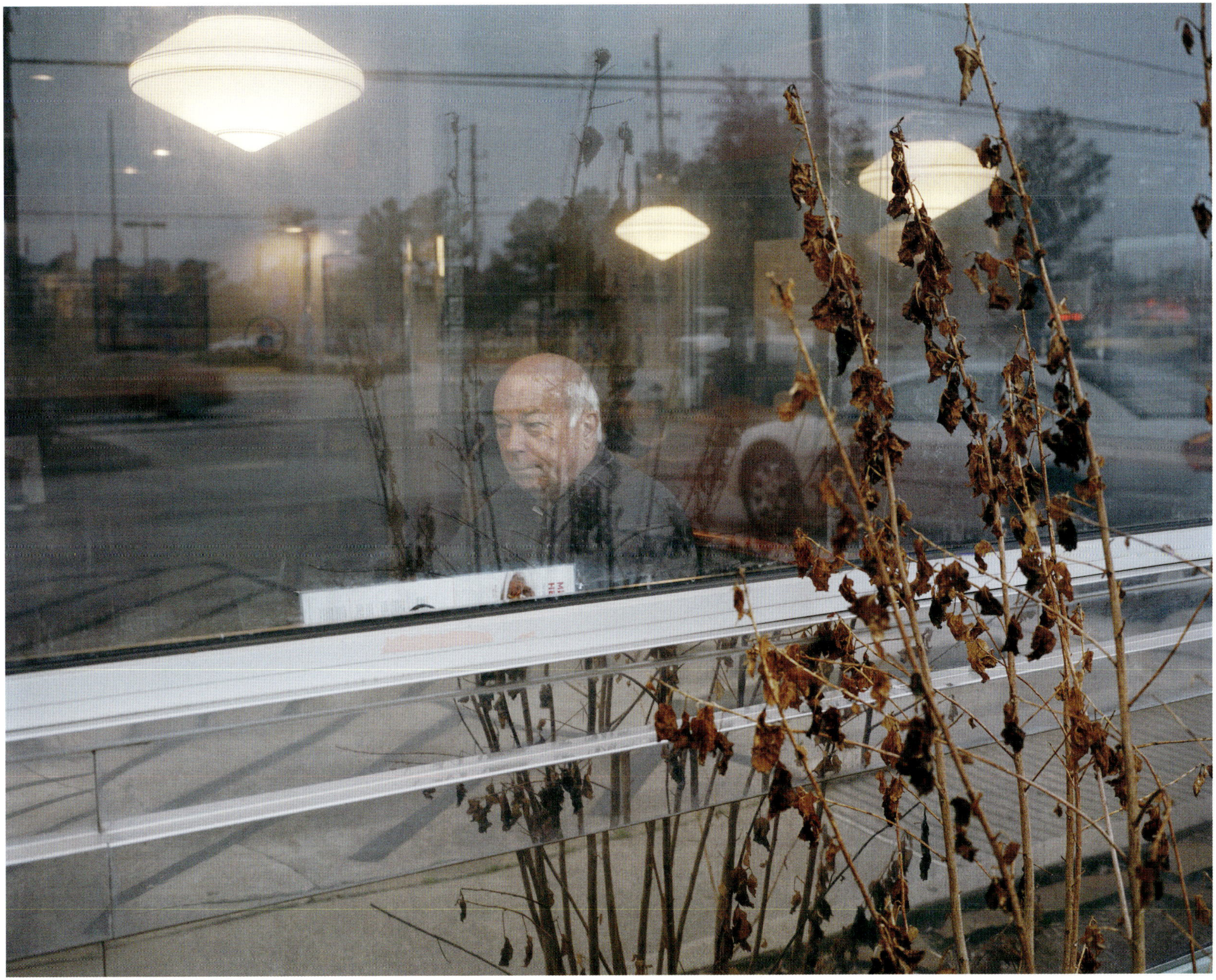

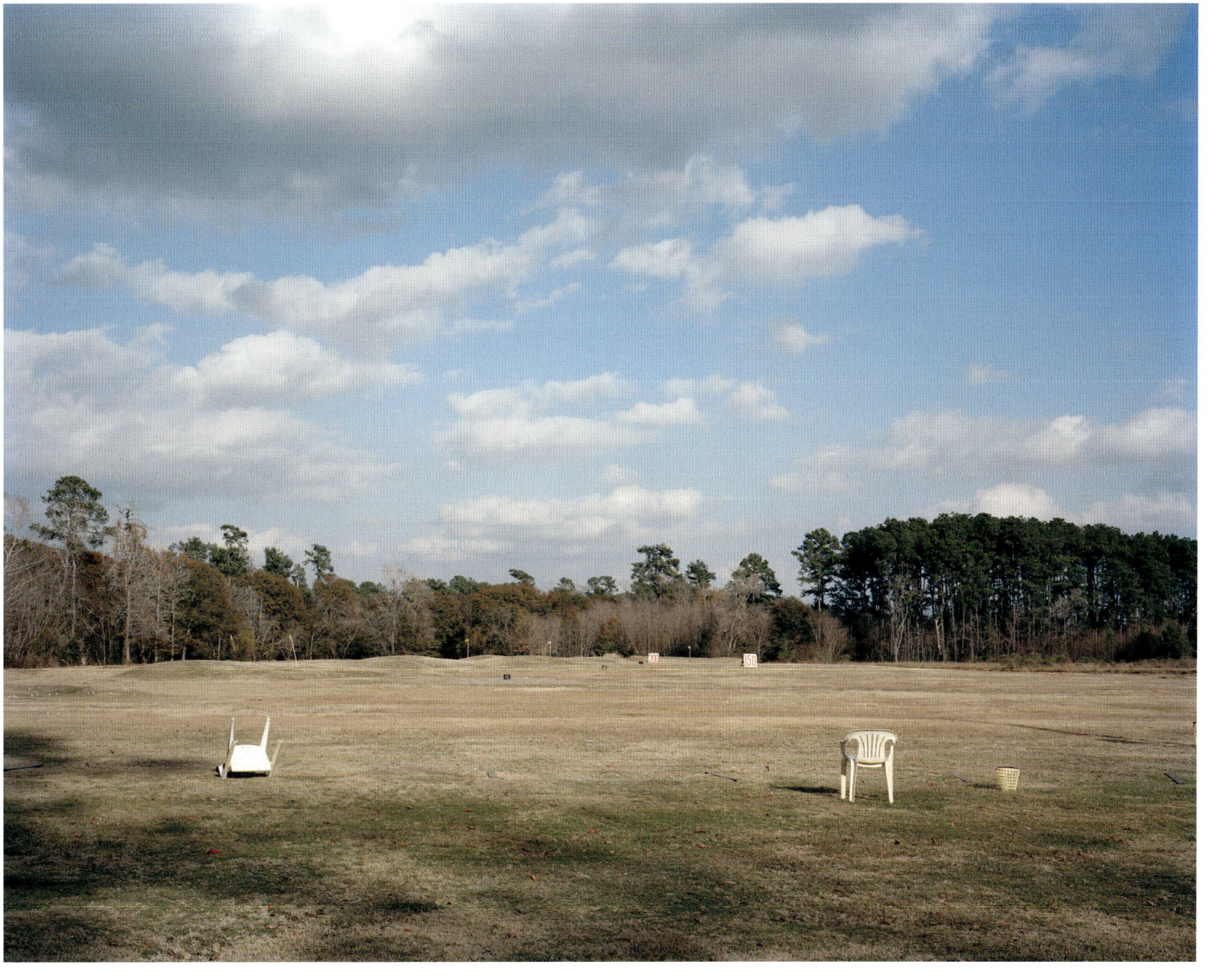
200
150

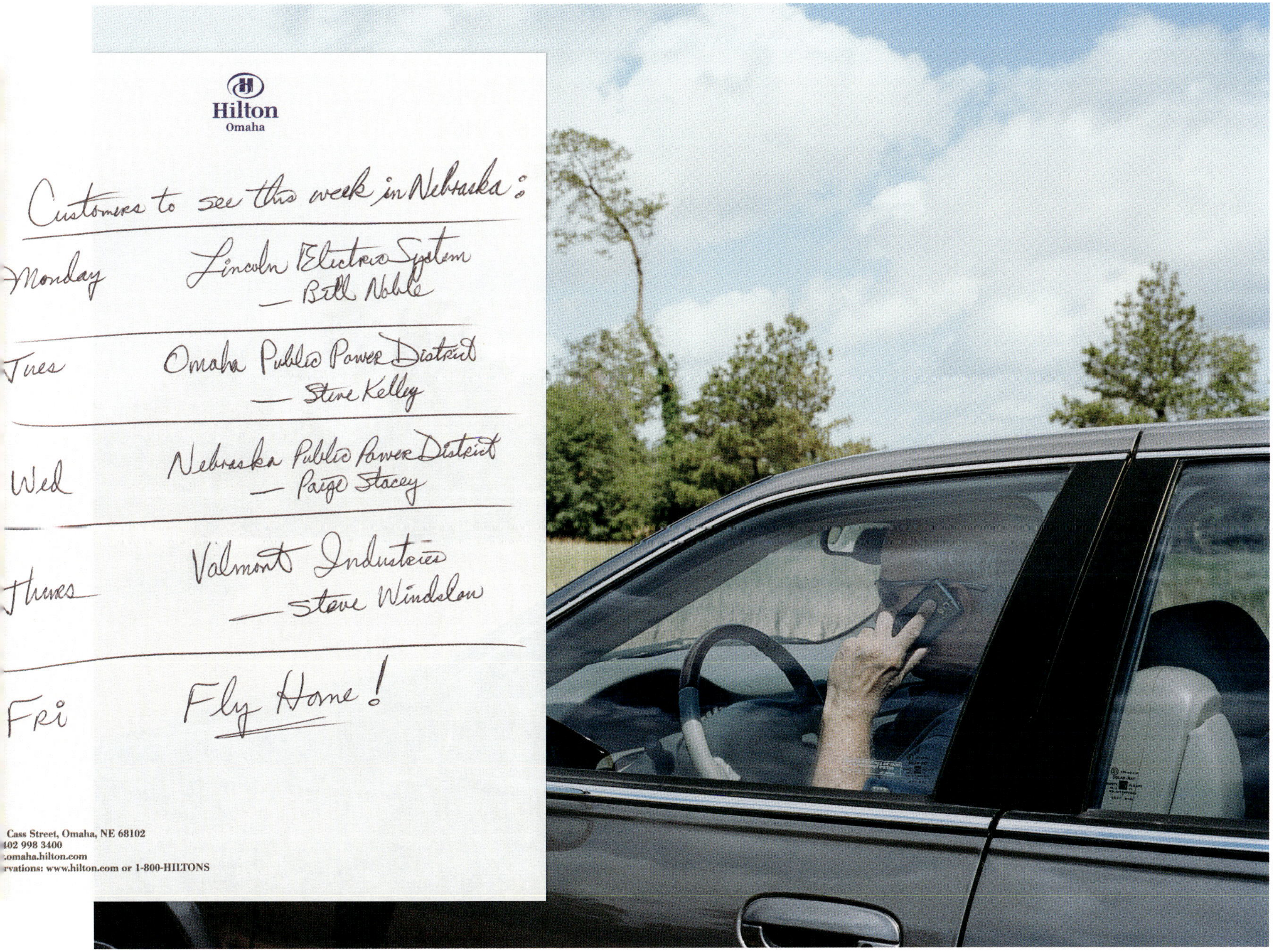
Hilton
Omaha
Customers to see this week in Nebraska:
Monday Lincoln Electric System
— Bill Noble
Tues Omaha Public Power District
— Steve Kelley
Wed Nebraska Public Power District
— Paige Stacey
Thurs Valmont Industries
— Steve Windslow
Fri Fly Home!
Cass Street, Omaha, NE 68102
402 998 3400
.omaha.hilton.com
rvations: www.hilton.com or 1-800-HILTONS

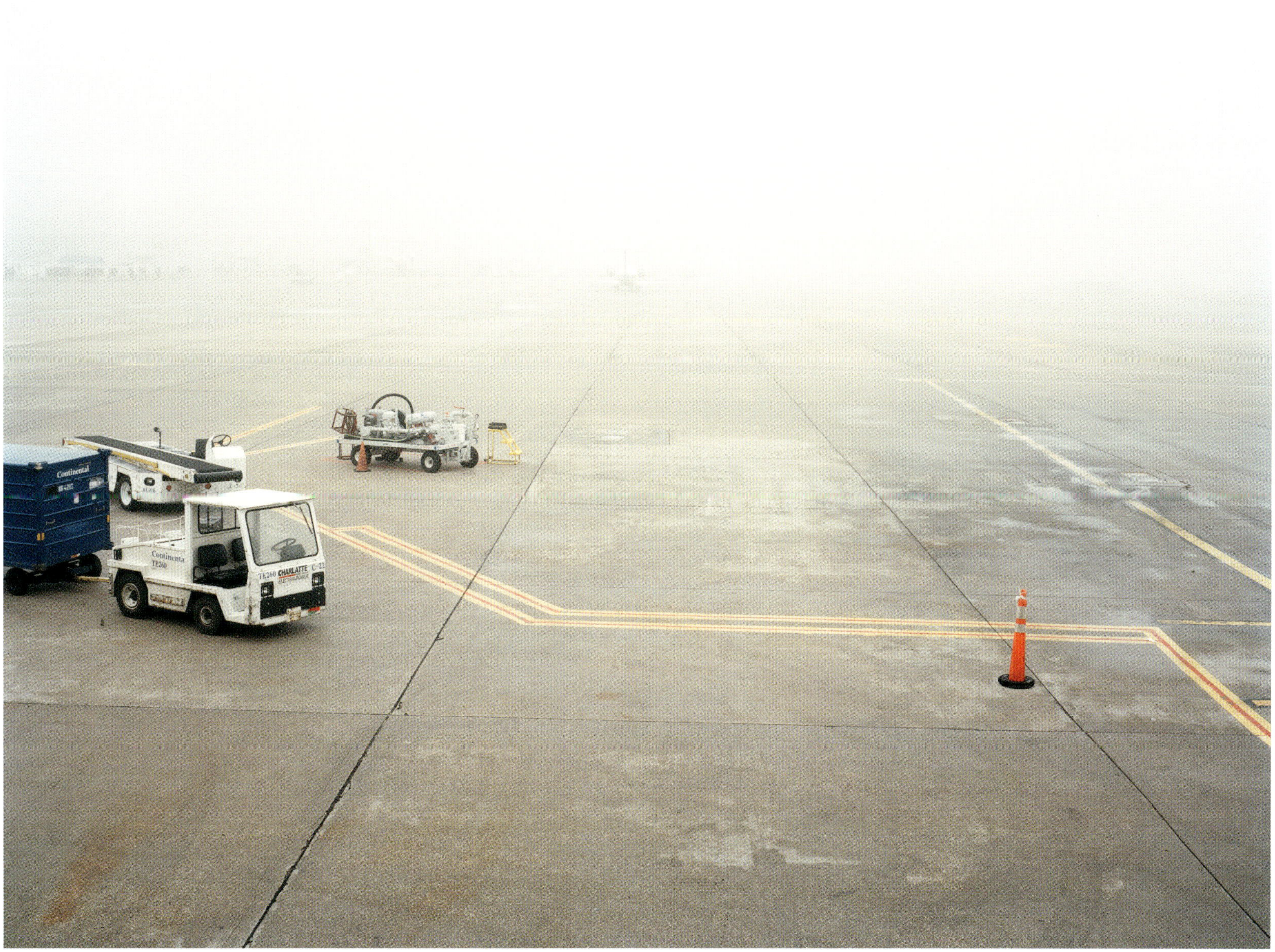
Continental
Continenta
TE260
CHARLATTE

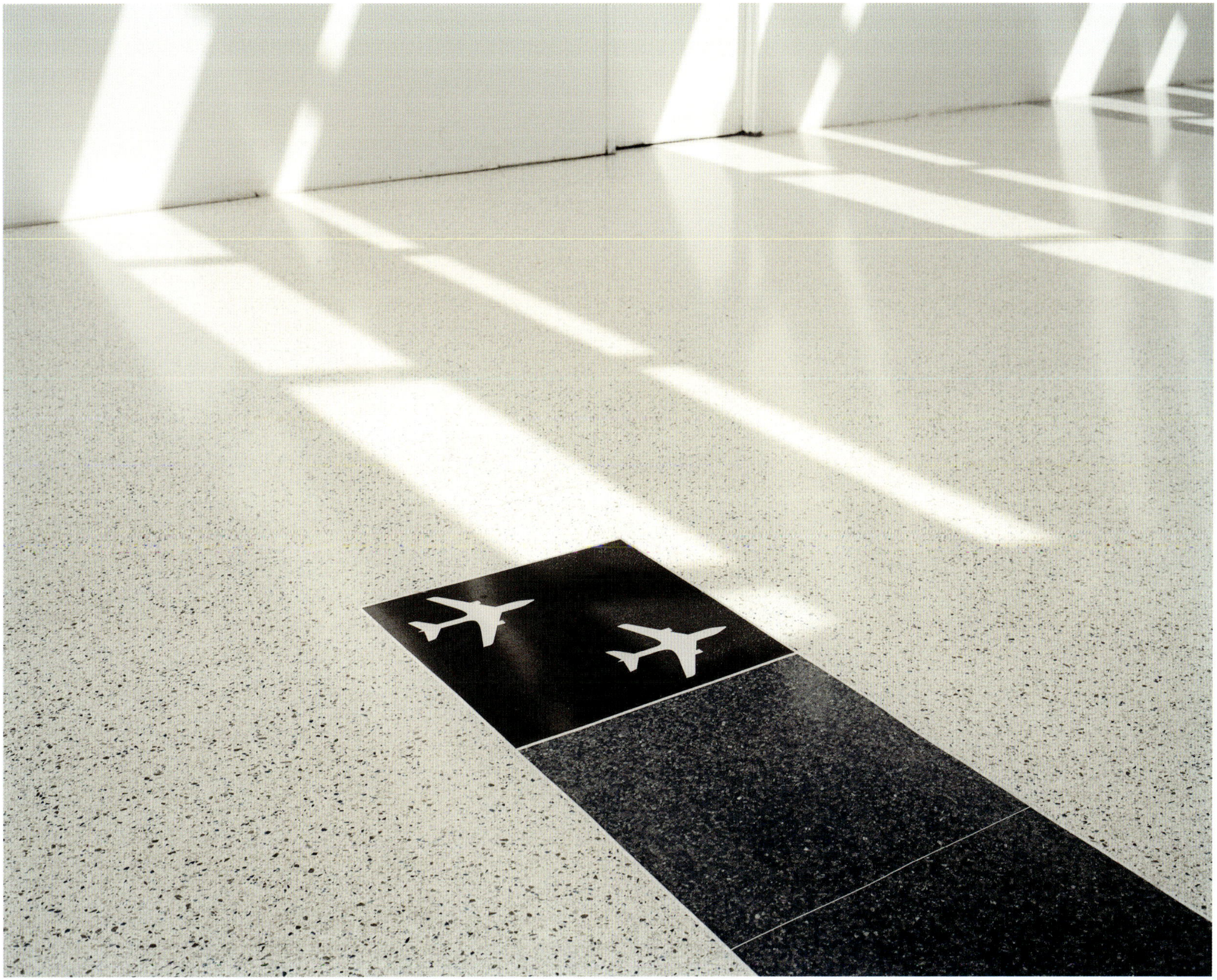

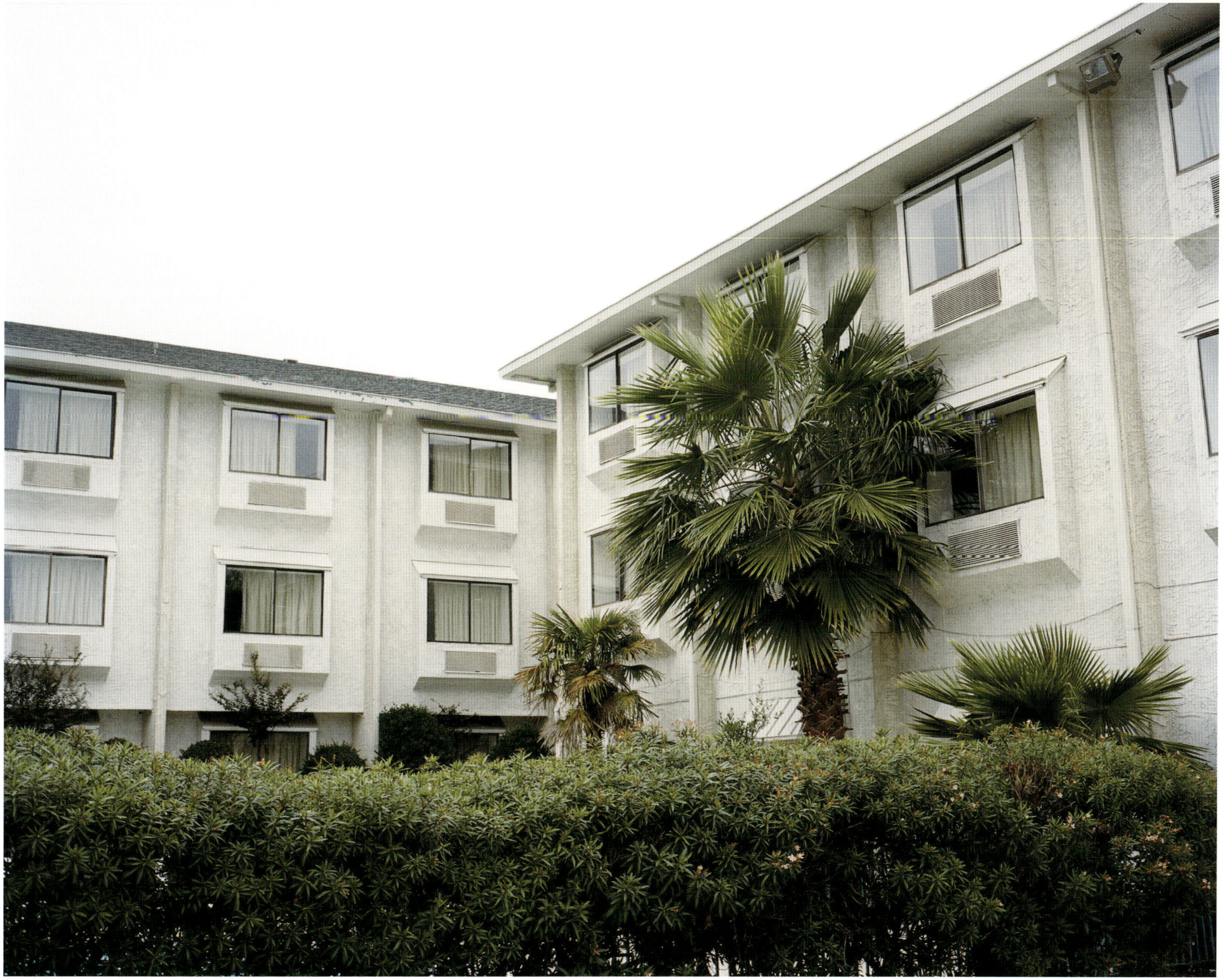

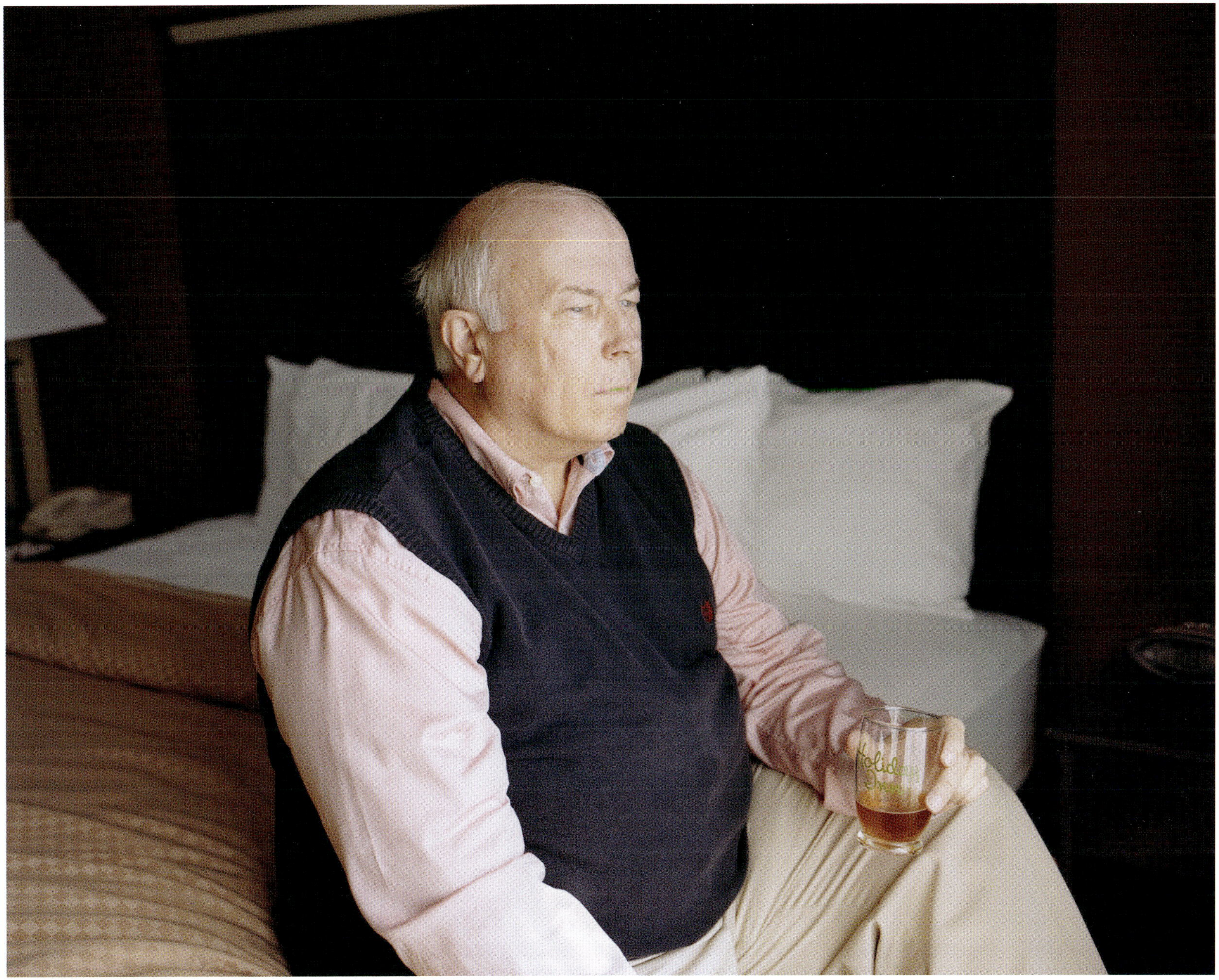
Holiday

Full Name:	Dennis Anthony Macel
Date of Birth:	2.20.1948
Occupation:	Regional Sales Manager, Treated Wood Industry
Miles Traveled by Plane in 2010:	8,500
Miles Traveled by Car in 2010:	6,000
Number of States Visited Last Month:	6
Number of States Visited in Career:	42
Approximate Number of Miles Traveled in Career:	7,000,000–8,000,000
Number of Membership Cards for Hotel Chains:	8
Number of Membership Cards for Rental Cars:	5
Total Revenue for Sales Last Year:	$6,000,000
Number of Companies Employed by in Career:	3
Number of Days Away from Home Last Year:	118
Memberships:	Knights of Columbus, Southern Pressure Treaters Association, American Wood Preservers Association, Utility Supply Management Association
Number of Company Cars Throughout Career:	12
Number of Cadillacs Personally Purchased:	1
Price of a Single Telephone Pole:	$550 for 1 Southern Yellow Pine, 40 ft.
Number of Poles Sold Per Year:	36,000
Total Career Sales, Telephone Poles:	1,500,000
Life Expectancy of a Telephone Pole:	35–40 years
Career-Span Expectancy of This Salesman:	44 years
Planned Year of Retirement:	2014
Years Married to My Mother:	35
Time Spent Away from Home in Career:	4,244 days or 11.62 years

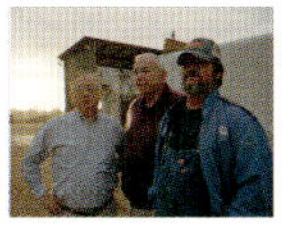
31
Charlie, Dad, and Larry,
Jasper, Texas

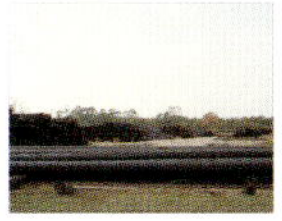
33
Southern Yellow Pines,
Jasper, Texas

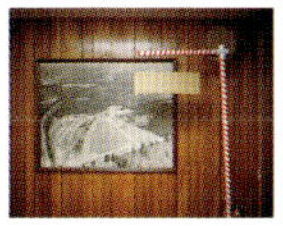
35
Aerial Photograph of Wood Treatment Plant,
Jasper, Texas

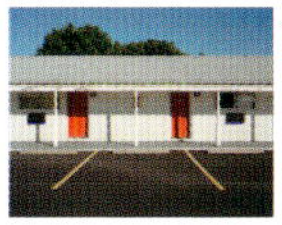
37
Sayville Motor Lodge,
Sayville, New York

Motel Notes No. 3,
Hampton Inn,
St. Louis, Missouri

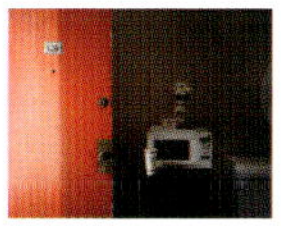
39
Room 126, Sayville Motor Lodge,
Sayville, New York

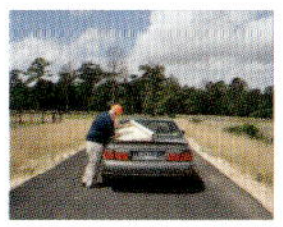
41
Surveying,
Tomball, Texas

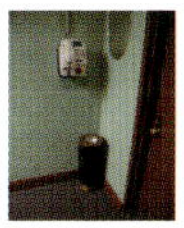
42
Days Inn,
Oklahoma City, Oklahoma

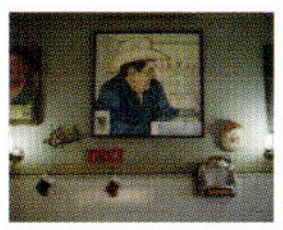
43
Cafe Texan,
Huntsville, Texas

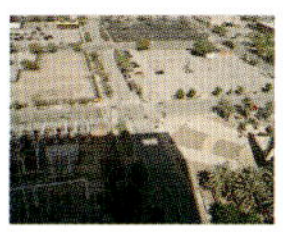
45
View Downtown from Convention
Center Marriott, Houston, Texas

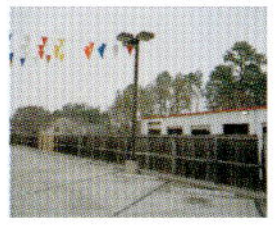
46
Parking Lot,
Spring, Texas

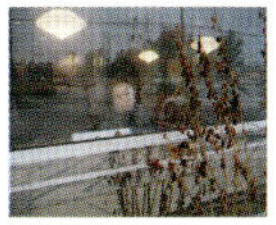
47
7:00 a.m., Denny's Breakfast,
Spring, Texas

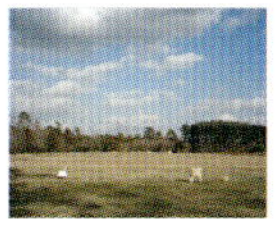
49
Driving Range,
Pearland, Texas

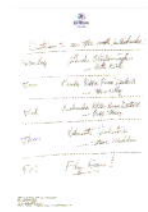
Motel Notes No. 4,
Hilton Hotel,
Omaha, Nebraska

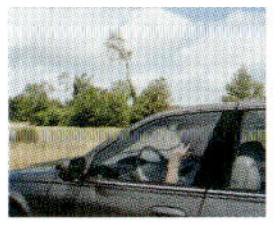
51
Roadside Conference Call
En Route to Spring, Texas

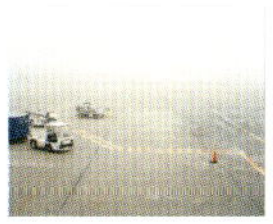
53
Foggy Runway, Will Rogers World Airport,
Oklahoma City, Oklahoma

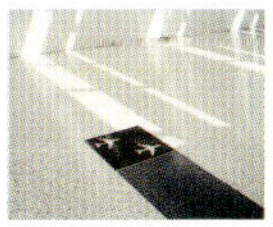
55
Terminal C, George Bush Intercontinental
Airport, Houston, Texas

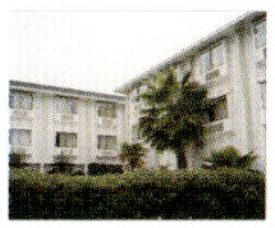
57
View from the Pool, Comfort Inn,
Little Rock, Arkansas

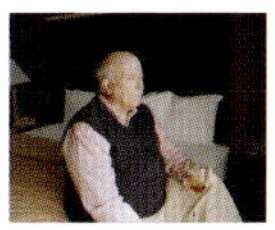
59
Dennis Anthony Macel,
Hitchcock, Texas

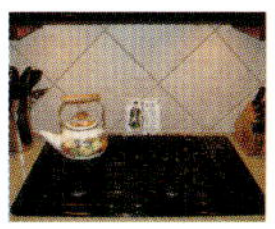
66
"May the Road Rise to Meet You,"
Spring, Texas
(*courtesy of Kathleen Macel*)

AFTERWORD

For the past forty years, my father has traveled around America as a telephone pole salesman. Dennis Macel is a man defined by his job and devoted to his family. Considering how much time he spent on the road, he was remarkably present during my childhood. Only occasionally did I really feel his absence. Over time I became more and more curious about where he went when his car pulled out of the driveway. When he announced to the family his plan to retire in a few years, I knew this could possibly be my only chance to get in the car with him.

The goal was to create a visual narrative of my father's professional life, separate from our shared family structure and experience. In the same way that a photo album functions to present an idealized version of a family's history, these photographs represent how my father and I want his working life to be remembered. Not in heroic terms, but something stoic and solitary. As such, the images are less about fact and more about a state of mind.

To tackle the enormous task of creating visual imagery to represent an entire life on the road, I retraced my father's steps, returning to destinations he had visited and photographing places he may have passed along the way. I also traveled with my father and documented him on the road in present day. In addition I collected ephemera from his home office, like handwritten notes on motel stationary and old snapshots.

We were traveling north on I-45 through Texas when I asked my dad what it is like dealing with customers. He told me: "There's that old saying that you don't know someone until you walk a few miles in their moccasins." It was in that spirit that I put myself in my father's own size 11 boots. Some scenes I photographed are based on stories he told me over the years or on notes I found in his files; others are a mixture of scenes from my imagination and portrayals of salesmen I've seen in movies and on television. Since little photographic evidence of my father's work life exists, popularized images of traveling businessmen worked to fill in the blanks.

Although my father was an active participant in this project, there were areas of his work life he would not allow me to photograph. For every room in his memory that he let me in, there was another I was left to imagine for myself. It is no coincidence that there are so many closed doors in these images. Often when we do see this man, he is in shadow or behind glass. His gaze is off in the distance. I see him, but does he see me?

On a larger scale, this project explores the changing nature of "the road" in American culture. As much as I am channeling the past through my father, I am also trailing the ghosts of earlier photographers. The genre of road-trip photography has been well explored by such giants as Robert Frank, Stephen Shore, Joel Sternfeld, and Alec Soth. Some of my favorite road photography projects were created by men and communicate a sense of freedom, masculinity, and wandering. Men taking to the road are typically on a quest. They become Huck Finn or Dean Moriarty. The woman on the road has been an anomaly. Our cultural lexicon still holds few references for the intrepid female explorer. There are, of course, exceptions like Justine Kurland with *This Train Is Bound for Glory*, wherein the road sings its reckless siren song in the form of a train whistle. Setting out alone on a journey to make photographs, I feel that sense of freedom and desire to throw caution to the wind, but there is also an unmistakable fog of vulnerability. That fear has, at times, held me back from getting the shot I want. It leaves me wondering how or whether the situation would differ were I a male photographer. The life and times of a traveling salesman is only half of this story. My father may be in front of the camera, but I am there too, representing my own half of the story behind the camera—appearing fleetingly in mirrors and shadow outlines—finding my own path down that lonely highway.

The story begins with a snapshot of my father as a young man leaving home in his company car and ends with a photograph of him in his sixties staring out a hotel window: an entire career condensed into a single business trip. In this parting image, we see him bathed in sunlight, sitting on the edge of a bed that is not his own. In his hand lies a cheap glass tumbler bought on eBay and given to him by me, his daughter and the photographer, moments before the shutter released. I handed him this prop because it bore the Holiday Inn logo I remember from when I was a kid and my father stayed only at Holiday Inns. The logo on the glass is synonymous with "Dad's away," "Dad's traveling." One of the reasons I became a photographer is because if you have a photograph of something, you can't forget or deny it. Every photograph says: "This existed." And now, at long last, after thirty years of this image existing only in my brain: here he sits on a hotel bed with a glass of whiskey in his hand, looking out the hotel window and thinking only of home as the shutter goes *click*.

When I started this project, I set out to rediscover my father as a man separate from his role in our family and to explore the sadness and the freedom of a life spent alone on the open highway. What I found in chasing this enormously elusive male figure is that I can never fully know my father or what it is like to be a man alone on the road.

In the end, this project became less about the American landscape or traveling salesmen or Robert Frank and more about distance: the emotional and physical distance between me and my dad, the vast expanses of land he travels to this day, and the memories of that brief stretch of time when we got to travel together.

— Sara Macel, 2013

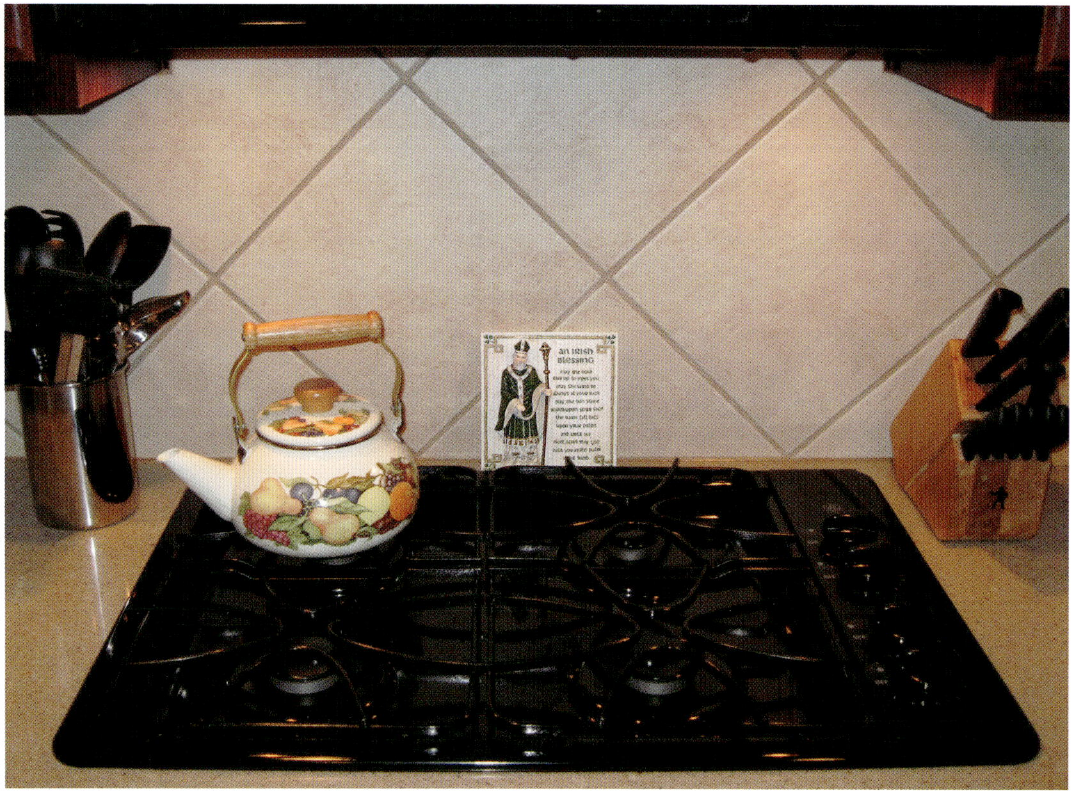
An Irish Blessing

ACKNOWLEDGMENTS

My dream of this book being published was realized thanks to Taj Forer and Michael Itkoff of Daylight Books. I am so grateful for their belief in this project and guidance in its creation.

Ursula Damm designed this book with elegance and precision. Thank you for being so open to my ideas and then making them better.

Special thanks to my mentor and friend Marvin Heiferman, whose beautiful words I could not be more honored to have on these pages.

Thank you to Sarah Charlesworth, Tina Barney, Charles Traub, Kiki Bauer, Gus Powell, Philip Perkis, Jeff Weiss, Elinor Carucci, Randy West, Lyle Rexer, Penelope Umbrico, Jan Avgikos, Bonnie Yochelson, Maureen Drennan, Matthew Baum, Seth Lambert, Nick Shepard, Matthew C. Lange, Nathan Ramirez, Chris Sellas, Adam Ryder, Corinne Schulze, Alex Severin, Michael Aghy, Chandra Glick, Carly Gaebe, James Pomerantz, Jenny Riffle, Liz Arenberg, Mia Baxter, Amani Willet, Rachel Styer, Alec Soth, Christian Patterson, Deb Willis, Tom Drysdale, Bruce and Emily Davidson, David Maloney, Kathryne Hall, Kris Graves, Ariel Shanberg, Larissa Leclair, Barbara Tannenbaum, David Bram, Jennifer Schwartz, Annick Sjobakken, Brandon Thibodeaux, Matthew Crowther, Elizabeth Fleming, Laura Nolden, Roy Flukinger, Bevin Bering Dubrowski, Fabiano Busdraghi, June Kim, Sean Carroll, Darius Himes, Mary Virginia Swanson, Harry Hardie, Dianne Timblin, and Sarah Simms for their insights and encouragement.

Thank you to the Aaron Siskind Foundation and the School of Visual Arts Alumni Society for their support in the creation of this work.

We met many kindhearted folks on our travels, but I especially want to thank Charles R. Faulds and Larry Carrell for their cameo appearances.

I am overwhelmed with love and thanks to my family: my mom, Kathleen Quinn Macel, for being the beacon that always guides our way home—1.4.3. And my beautiful sisters, Andrea and Connie, who patiently indulge me every time I ask them to pull over so I can make a photograph. Thank you to my beautiful Gram-Rita for keeping us all on the straight and narrow. And thank you to the hand in my glove, Michael. You're true blue, Catanese.

This project would not exist without the love and support of my muse and collaborator Dennis Macel. You're the best, Dad. This one's for you.

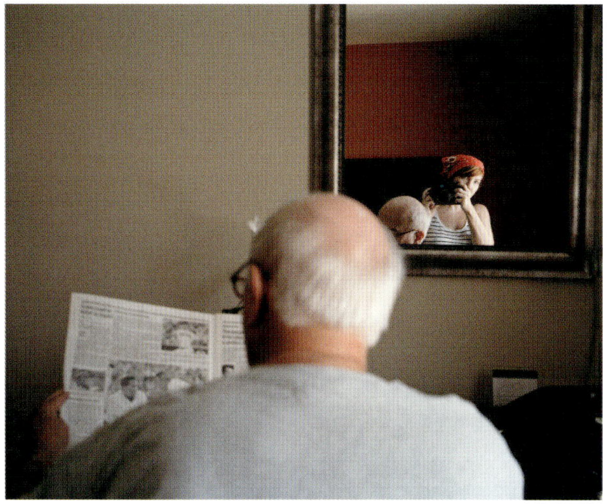

For my father, Dennis

May the road rise to meet you.
May the wind be always at your back.
May the sun shine warm upon your face,
The rains fall soft upon your fields.
And until we meet again,
May God hold you in the palm of His hand.

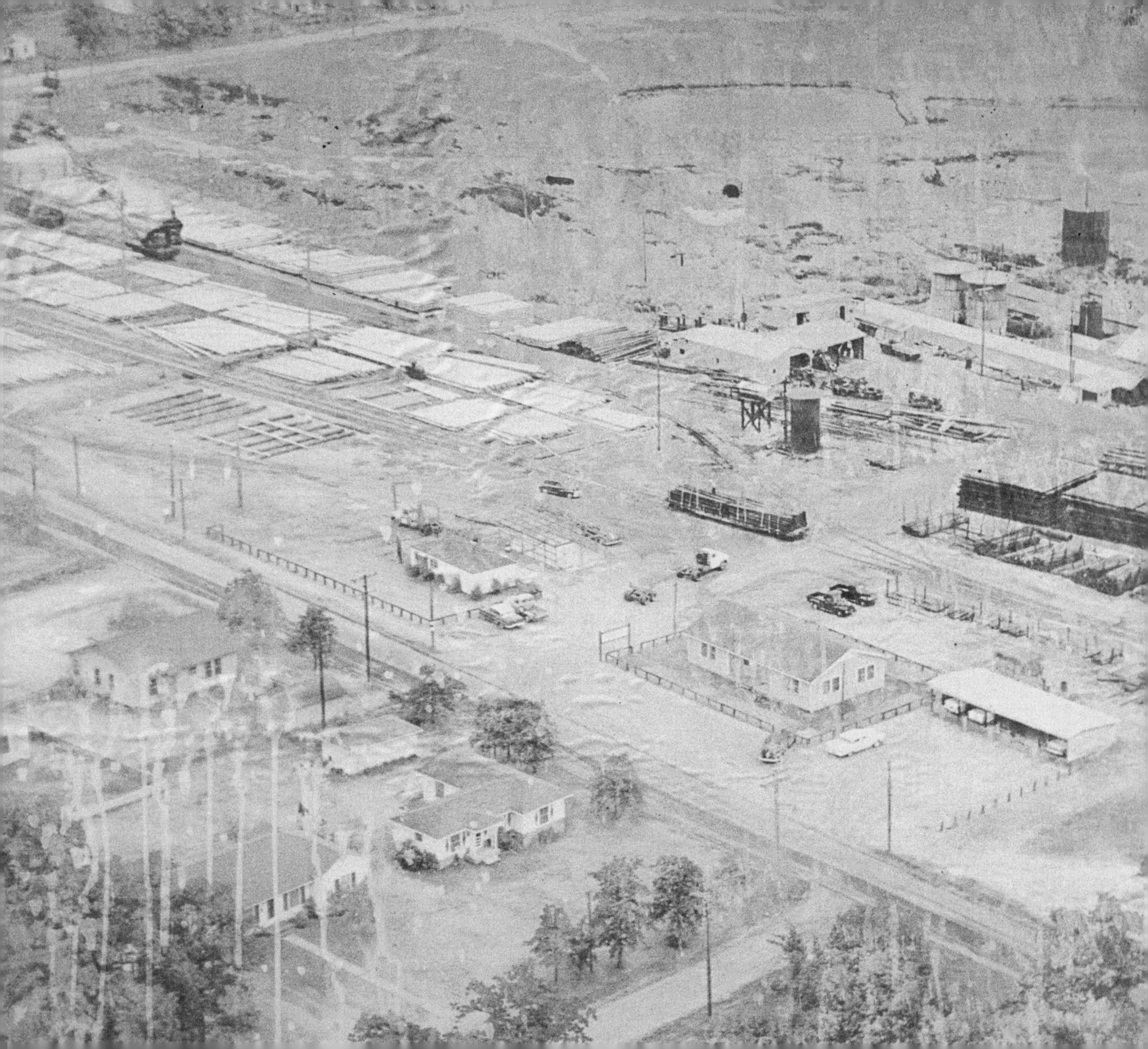